SENIOR MIND GYM

PUZZLES TO EXERCISE THE BRAIN

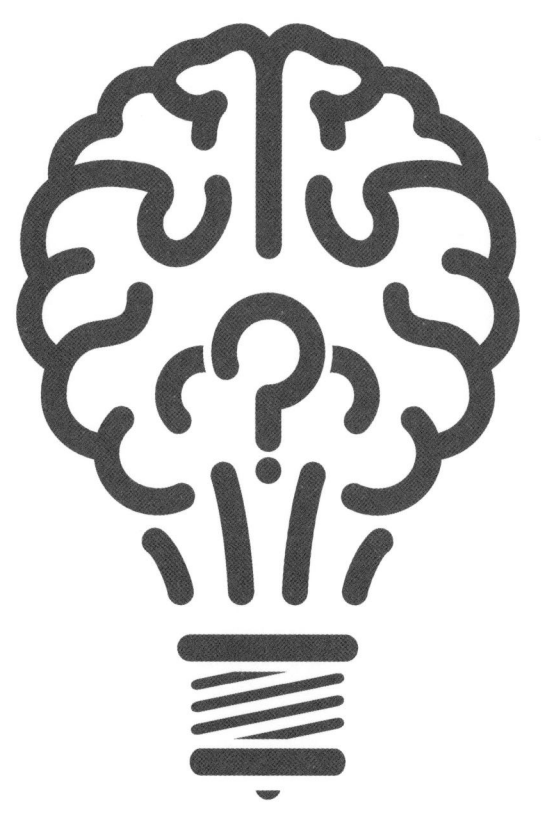

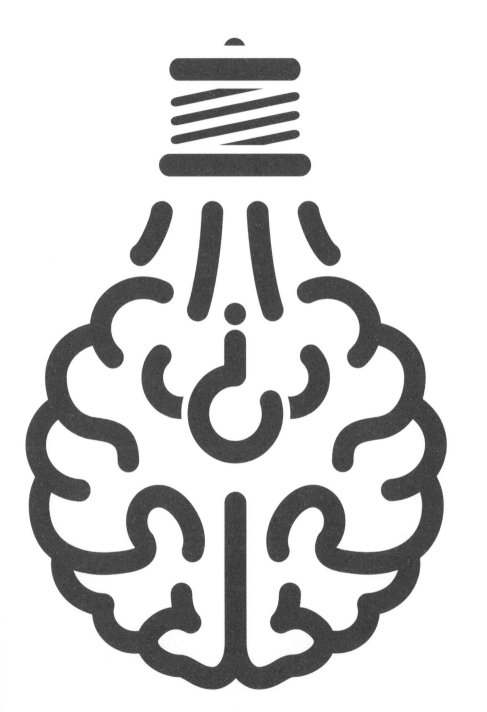

SENIOR MIND GYM

PUZZLES TO EXERCISE THE BRAIN

AMMONITE
PRESS

KRISTY McGOWAN

INTRODUCTION

Get ready for a workout! This book will challenge your brain, increase your mental flexibility, boost your problem-solving skills, and entertain you at the same time. Inside, you will find familiar puzzles such as crosswords, word searches, sudokus, and quizzes. You will also discover puzzles you've probably never seen before. It's always fun to come across something different.

Studies show that novelty is good for the brain. Spending as little as just 15 minutes on something new every day can build mental connections. These new pathways can then boost your problem-solving skills in other tasks. It seems that humans are hardwired to seek novelty, in part because our brains crave it. A good way to satisfy that craving is by playing.

In fact, our history with games stretches back a long way—in Jordan, there is evidence of mancala, the "seed sowing" game, dated to around 6,000 years ago. Games promote social interaction, build teams, and strengthen bonds between people. Like all games, puzzles mirror and allow people to practice techniques that are needed in the real world, such as strategy, planning, and creativity.

To solve the puzzles in this book, you will have to use skills such as recalling memories, employing lateral thinking, anagramming, logic, word-building, and practical reasoning. Some of the puzzles are very straightforward and others will test your patience. You'll learn facts you never knew. You will say, "Aha!" And, hopefully, you will smile.

The mind is just like a muscle: the more you exercise it, the stronger it gets, and the more it can expand.

—Idowu Koyenikan

Puzzle-solving is like any skill: learn how, practice, and you'll get better. As you improve, you'll become wiser to the tricks that the puzzle-writer uses to try to fool you. For example, a crossword clue for a three-letter answer might say, "The middle of water?" The question mark is a hint that the answer is unusual somehow, but how? The clue could refer to H_2O, the formula for water. In which case, the answer could be TWO. Or, it could be referring to the word "water" itself. The middle letter of water is TEE. Either way, the first letter of the answer is "T" and you're off to the next clue. Once you start considering seemingly impenetrable clues like this one in a new way, you'll cruise through crosswords. Just like any exercise, the more you do it, the easier it will get.

The brain needs exercise the same way your body does. Give it a good workout and you can keep your brain young, flexible, creative, and adaptable. Just 15 minutes a day of a fun workout will reward you with a healthier, stronger brain.

You'll see that the puzzles are marked with weights to show you the difficulty of each one. Do a lightweight puzzle for an easy workout or choose one with three weights for a puzzle with more "crunch." This is a variety book, so find your favorite kind of puzzle and start there. If you're having trouble with a type of puzzle you aren't familiar with, find the easy version and try that. There is nothing routine about the exercise you'll get in this book. There are a lot of different types of puzzles—and more than 100 to try!

You can find the answers to all the puzzles on pages 116–125.

LET'S
BEGIN

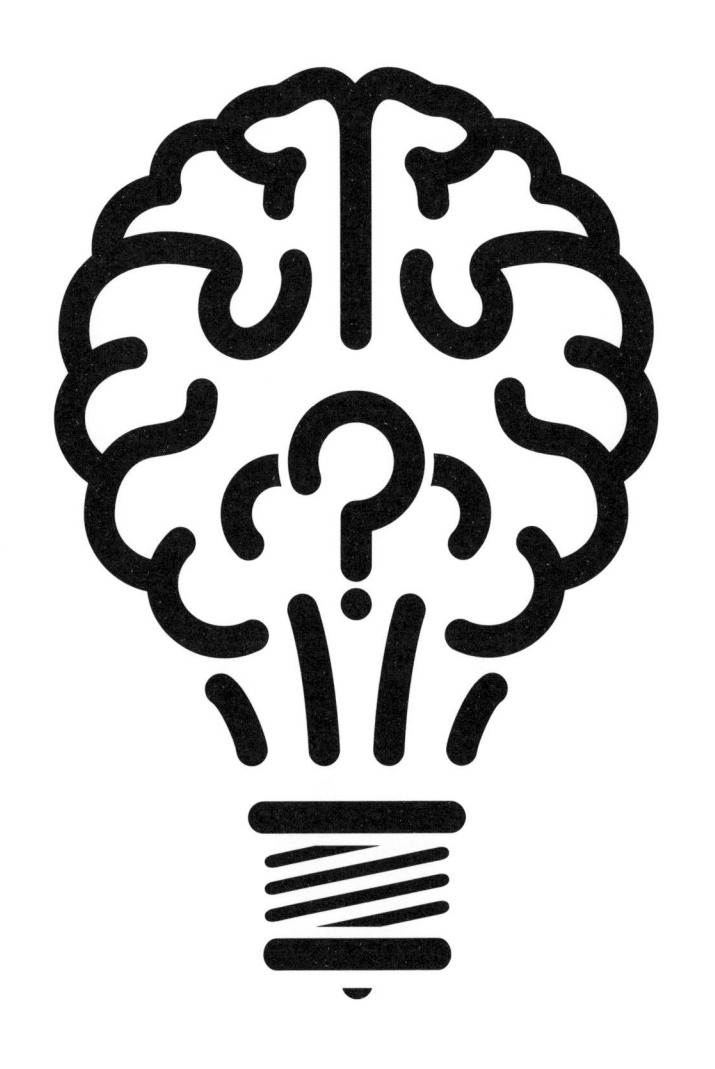

TRIVIA
MATCHING

Starting at the top of the left-hand column and working your way down, reunite the famous couples by drawing a line to join the dots next to each name. You may want to use a ruler! When you're done, read the letters you've crossed, in the order you crossed them, to find a phrase.

ANSWER ....

CROSSWORD
PRIMER

Always hated crosswords because they seem impossible to start? Here are three fun and quick crosswords. If you don't know the answer to 1-Across, keep reading until you can get an answer. Fill-in-the-blanks-style clues can be a good way to get a foothold on any crossword. If you already like to do crosswords, try to solve these in less than a minute.

ACROSS
1 Feline
4 Mining mineral
5 Marry

DOWN
1 Bovine
2 "_____ we there yet?"
3 Danson of *Cheers*

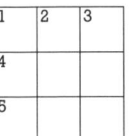

ACROSS
1 Pooch
4 Spanish year
5 _____ and breakfast

DOWN
1 Tiny bit
2 Only
3 Neptune or Thor

ACROSS
1 Picnic invader
4 Ghost noise
5 It sounds like you

DOWN
1 Homer Simpson's dad
2 Right away
3 Foot digit

SMART TIP

Doing anything novel is a good way to give your brain a workout. So, travel home by a different route or brush your teeth with the opposite hand to normal. Making little changes to your routine might lead to fun surprises, too.

FLOWERY
CROSSWORD

ACROSS

1 National symbol
5 "She loves me not" piece
10 Light red
14 Olympics sled event
15 "I never met ___ didn't like" (3 words)
16 Key with one sharp: abbr.
17 Lumberjack
18 Brunch time, maybe
19 Corn bread
20 Purple-blue
22 Rational
23 Fishing poles
24 Like old records or floor covering
25 Donald Duck's girlfriend
29 Suffix for mart or lingu
31 As well
32 Supermarket or theater walkways
35 _____ on a Grecian urn
38 Low-growing flower, also known as may bells
41 5G_____: mobile phone standard
42 Roof of the mouth
43 Doing nothing
44 Web address
45 Flat-topped hills
46 Water flower
50 Terrible fate
53 Unsigned, abbr.
54 Finger-clicking, fire-breathing plant?
60 Prefix meaning "half"
61 Wanderer
62 Lost fish in a Pixar film
63 Coup d'_____
64 Ring-shaped coral island
65 Astronauts' orange drink
66 Got up

67 Johnny-jump-up, e.g.
68 Part of the eye

DOWN

1 Flutter
2 Swanky
3 Teen or Golden follower
4 Spice Girl Halliwell
5 Lanai
6 Redact
7 Army vehicles with treads
8 Overly fussy
9 Green citrus fruit
10 Coke competitor
11 "So why on earth should _____" (lyric from *A Hard Day's Night*) (2 words)
12 Nincompoop
13 Prepare to be knighted
21 Dryly humorous
24 Passport document or credit card
25 A kind of bighorn sheep in Alaska
26 Lightly touched down
27 Small island
28 Tofu source
29 "Before _____ you go..." (2 words)
30 Actress Campbell
32 At a distance
33 "_____ never work!"
34 _____ Na Na
35 Pioneer automaker
36 Oscar _____ Renta (2 words)
37 Baby blues
39 Magnum _____
40 Untruth
45 Three-part vaccine given to kids, abbr.

1	2	3	4		5	6	7	8	9		10	11	12	13
14					15						16			
17					18						19			
20				21							22			
			23						24				
25	26	27	28				29	30					
31					32	33	34				35	36	37
38			39						40				
41				42						43			
			44				45					
46	47	48	49			50	51	52				
53				54	55				56	57	58	59
60			61						62			
63			64						65			
66			67						68			

46 Light beam
47 _____ a customer (2 words)
48 Noted cartoon tank engine, in Spanish language editions
49 Couple together
50 Matt of *The Martian*
51 Australian gems
52 In an unusual way

54 Fastener
55 "_____ chance!" (2 words)
56 Opposed to
57 Equipment
58 Prefix for present or potent
59 Eggy Christmas drinks

SHAKESPEARE
CRISSCROSS

Fit the names of the Shakespearean characters into the grid.

ARIEL	JULIET CAPULET	PROSPERO
BEATRICE	JULIUS CAESAR	PUCK
CLEOPATRA	KING CLAUDIUS	ROMEO MONTAGUE
DOGBERRY	KING LEAR	ROSALIND
DON JOHN	MACBETH	TITANIA
EDMUND	MARC ANTONY	TITUS ANDRONICUS
EMILIA	MERCUTIO	TYBALT
HERO	OPHELIA	YORICK
IAGO	OTHELLO	
JACQUES	PRINCE HAMLET	

CIRCULAR
FILL IN THE BLANKS

To solve these puzzles, add a letter to the blank space in each circle to make a six-letter word. You'll have to figure out whether the word is winding around in a clockwise or counterclockwise direction. And you'll have to decide where the word starts within the circle. To aid in solving, the letters that you fill in will also spell a six-letter word.

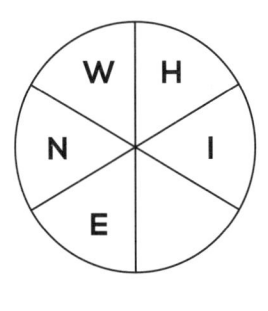
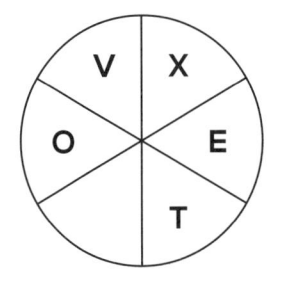
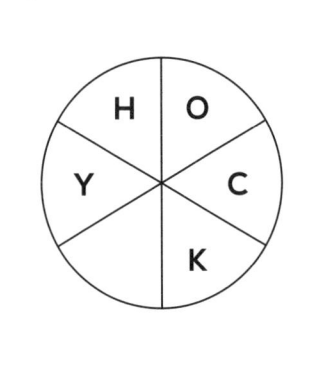

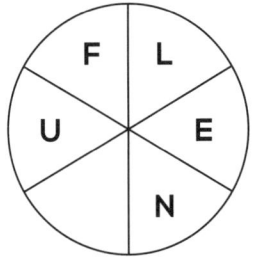
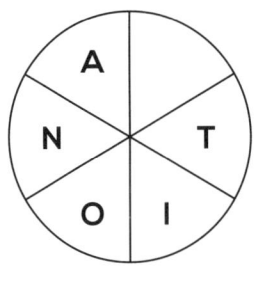
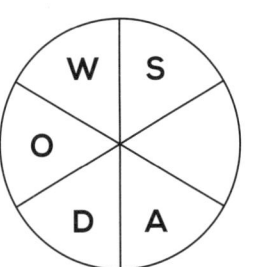

SIX-LETTER WORD . . . .

SMART TIP

When you want to remember something you've just heard, read, or thought about, try repeating it out loud.

ANIMAL
WORD SEARCH

In this word search you'll be looking for cryptids—secretive creatures that may or may not exist. See how many you can find! When you're done, read the leftover letters for an additional message.

```
                        I W A I
                      L Y G H W T K
                    J A L O 👁 G E E
                    E K O P W N Y R
                  B R E C O O I
                  E S E H G E M E S
                R A E R N O
                E S Y I E A
                L T D E S D
              W O E M S N
              O F V O M O
              H B I N O C
              E K O L S N A
          T O O F G I B R D A T S G
        C H U P A C A B R A M M E T E
      N H O N N A M D R A Z I L R E M
      E E S P N O G A R D O N S O R B
      K S A M L A T M O T H M A N E R
      A S S A E I S S E T E O H A T R
      R I O H A W A T E R H O U N D
      K E H C T A U Q S A S R M
```

ALMAS
BEAST OF BODMIN
    MOOR
BIGFOOT
BROSNO DRAGON
CHAMP
CHESSIE
CHUPACABRA
DINGONEK

IGOPOGO
JERSEY DEVIL
KRAKEN
LAKE ERIE MONSTER
LIZARD MAN
LOCH NESS MONSTER
MEGACONDA
MINGWA
MOTHMAN

OZARK HOWLER
SASQUATCH
TAHOE TESSIE
WATER HOUND
YETI
YOWIE

OFFICE
LOGIC PUZZLE

Here is a tough real-world logic puzzle. Your company has a new office. It has eight offices that go in a square around a large courtyard. They are numbered 1–8, with the 1 starting in the northwest corner and proceeding clockwise around the courtyard. Your executives—Angelina, Bruno, Cassidy, Dean, Eva, Freddy, Gina, and Henry— have told you their preferences in where their offices are located. Can you find a solution that will make them all happy?

1	2	3
....	....	....
8		4
....		....
7	6	5
....	....	....

1 Freddy's favorite number is 7.
2 Gina and Bruno want corner offices, but Bruno wants to be in office 1.
3 Cassidy wants the northeast corner so she is closer to the door.
4 Henry is superstitious and wants an even-numbered office with the highest number possible.

5 Angelina wants office 8 because of its nice view.
6 Dean works closely with Gina and Cassidy and wants to be between them.
7 Henry wants to be across from Eva because they don't get along.

INSTRUMENTS
QUIZ

1 The most popular instrument to learn is the:
   a Piano   **b** Electric guitar   **c** Trumpet   **d** Flute

2 A Celtic bowed lyre called a crwth is from:
   a Wales   **b** Scotland   **c** England   **d** Ireland

3 The Glass Armonica was invented by which founder of the United States:
   a George Washington   **b** Sam Adams   **c** John Adams   **d** Benjamin Franklin

4 True or False: There's a 3.5-acre (1.4-hectare) cavern in Virginia with tuned stalactites that is the world's largest instrument.

5 True or False: A lithophone is a xylophone made of stones.

6 True or False: A zeusaphone, which creates sound from musical lightning, uses batteries for its energy.

7 True or False: The steel drum (or steel pan) is the only acoustic, non-electric instrument invented in the 20th century.

8 Didgeridoos are instruments created by indigenous people from:
   a South Africa   **b** Albania   **c** New Zealand   **d** Australia

9 The largest flute in existence has 18 feet (5.5m) of tubing and is called a:
   a Sousaphone   **b** Seussaphone   **c** Double contrabass flute   **d** Tuba

10 Stradivarius violins are famous for their mellow sound. They are made from three main woods: spruce, willow, and…
   a Maple   **b** Ash   **c** Elm   **d** Cedar

NAME
THE OBJECTS

EASY

Here are some oddly named objects. See how many you can name. When you're done, read down the first letter of each to name another object.

....

....

....

....

....

....

....

OBJECT ....

HAWAIIAN
ETYMOLOGY

Hawaiian is a beautiful language, and so many of its words are interesting combinations. Using the glossary provided, can you write the correct English word from the list below next to its Hawaiian counterpart on the opposite page?

GLOSSARY

a'o	teaching
ho'o	cause
kahua	place
kanaka	person
ki'i	picture
lele	fly
leka	letter
leo	voice
lolo	brain
mana'o	thought
mea	thing
pa'ani	fun
pahu	box
pa'i	snap
pepa	paper
pua'i	flow
uila	electric
'uiki	glimmer

ENGLISH WORDS

Angel
Brainstorm
Cardboard box
Computer
Email
Fuse box
Lightning
Microphone
Enlarge a photo
Playground
Projector
Radio
Take a photo
Toy box

SMART TIP

They say you are what you eat, so make sure you're chewing on the right things to keep your brain healthy. Salmon, eggs, broccoli, oranges, and blueberries all contain nutrients that will give your brain, as well as your body, a boost.

HARD

HAWAIIAN WORDS

mea ho'o lele leo …………………………………………

ki'i ho'o lele …………………………………………

pa'i ki'i …………………………………………

leka uila …………………………………………

kanaka lele …………………………………………

mea ho'o lele ki'i …………………………………………

kahua pa'ani …………………………………………

pahu pepa …………………………………………

pahu ho'o lele leo …………………………………………

pahu mea pa'ani …………………………………………

pua'i mana'o …………………………………………

pahu 'uiki uila …………………………………………

lolo uila …………………………………………

ho'o uila …………………………………………

FACE CARDS
CROSSWORD

ACROSS

1 Links org.
4 Inscribed pillar
9 Theme of this puzzle
14 Not 'neath
15 Consumed
16 January in Spain
17 Opposite of WSW
18 Give off
19 Jargon
20 Guys
21 Very large treasure
23 Male deer
25 Coup d' _____
26 Atmosphere
29 Go back and forth
34 Daughter of Tsar Nicholas
40 Evening, in ads
41 Handy multitasker
44 Paris pal
45 Arrangement, as of furniture
46 Sale indicator
49 French Mrs.
50 US state just east of Montana, for short
53 Shoe part
57 Marquis of _____ Rules, in boxing
64 Leg, in slang
65 Prefix for violet or conservative
66 At right angles to the keel
67 Ambient music's Brian
68 Total (2 words)
69 Gin's partner
70 "To be or _____ to be…"
71 _____ in comparison
72 Terrible African virus
73 Golf peg

DOWN

1 Verses
2 Civet's cousin
3 Sports venue
4 Look for
5 Yellow or black cab
6 Vingt-_____ (gambling game) (2 words)
7 Shelf
8 Build _____ egg: save (2 words)
9 Divulge
10 Getting _____ years (2 words)
11 Cravings
12 Jason's ship
13 Weaving frame
22 _____ in rabbit (2 words)
24 Blow a _____
27 "Who am _____ judge?" (2 words)
28 UK fliers
30 Tooth material
31 Flank
32 "Got two fives for _____?" (2 words)
33 Sunset direction
34 Slightly open
35 Identify
36 Amino _____
37 Sticky stuff
38 Unwell
39 Pie _____ mode (2 words)
42 US TV network that shows old movies
43 Dreaming sleep phase, abbr.
47 Yearly records
48 Dept. store stock
51 Diminish
52 Meat dish on a stick
54 James Bond, e.g.
55 Kayak's cousin

56 Overact
57 Witty remark
58 Radius' neighbor
59 Bibliography abbr. (2 words)
60 Writer _____ Stanley Gardner

61 Nevada gambling city
62 Train track
63 Village People hit

GEOGRAPHY
QUIZ

1 What river flows through Victoria Falls, the largest waterfall in the world?
   a Zambezi   **b** Congo   **c** Nile   **d** Niger

2 The largest natural deepwater bay in the world by water volume, Guanabara Bay, is ringed by beautiful mountains. It has a more famous name. What is it?
   a Cape Town   **b** San Francisco Bay   **c** Rio de Janeiro   **d** Manila Bay

3 With over 37 million occupants, what is the largest city in the world?
   a Sao Paulo   **b** Delhi   **c** Shanghai   **d** Tokyo

4 The longest river in the world is the Nile, which stretches from Ethiopia and Tanzania all the way to the Mediterranean on Egypt's delta. About how long is it?
   a 2,000 miles (3,219km)   **b** 1,500 miles (2,414km)   **c** 4,000 miles (6,437km)
   d 3,000 miles (4,828km)

5 The largest country by area is Russia. It spans from the Baltic Sea all the way to the Pacific. How many different time zones are there to cover this expanse?
   a 6   **b** 11   **c** 9   **d** 13

6 What country has the highest average elevation at 10,760 feet (3,280m)?
   a Kyrgyzstan   **b** Bhutan   **c** Tajikistan   **d** Nepal

7 What country has the lowest average elevation—only 6 feet (1.8m)?
   a Maldives   **b** Qatar   **c** The Netherlands   **d** Denmark

8 The smallest country at less than a square mile (2.6km^2), Vatican City is entirely surrounded by the city of Rome and the country of Italy. Also less than a square mile and surrounded by another country, what is the second smallest country?
   a Bahrain   **b** Liechtenstein   **c** Monaco   **d** San Marino

9 At over 450 feet (137m) tall, what is the tallest pyramid built in ancient times?
   a Xi'an Pyramid, China   **b** Pyramid of the Sun, Mexico   **c** Tikal, Guatemala
   d Great Pyramid of Giza, Egypt

10 The Mongol Empire controlled over 9 million square miles (over 23,000,000km^2) in the late 1200s. But which empire controlled even more, over 13 million square miles (nearly 34,000,000km^2), in 1920?
   a Russian   **b** British   **c** Qing   **d** Spanish

The nice thing about doing a crossword puzzle is, you know there is a solution.

—Stephen Sondheim

HARD

SAME LETTER
START "M"

Answer as many of these six-letter words that begin with "M" as you can. For an extra challenge, give yourself a time limit. When you're done, read down the highlighted diagonal for another six-letter "M" word.

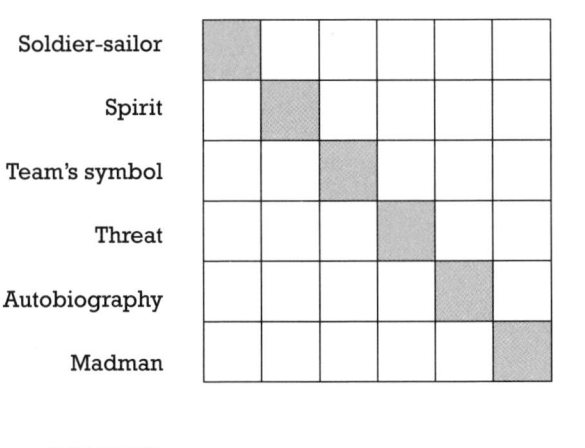

Soldier-sailor

Spirit

Team's symbol

Threat

Autobiography

Madman

"M" WORD ....

SMART TIP

Making up a mnemonic is a creative way to remember a list. They can be acronyms (such as RICE to remember Rest, Ice, Compression, and Elevation for injured limbs) or sentences (such as Richard Of York Gave Battle In Vain to remember the shades of the rainbow). Try making one up to remember your list next time you go shopping.

ESCAPE
THE PAGE

Make your way through the maze from the top to the bottom. When you find the correct path, use the numbers on the path as your exit code.

IN

2
0
5
9
2
6
4
7
1
3
8

EXIT CODE

OUT

NUMBERS
CRYPTOGRAM

This is a simple substitution cryptogram using numbers. The answer is a quote by a famous person.

A	B	C	D	E	F	G	H	I	J	K	L	M	N	O	P	Q	R	S	T	U	V	W	X	Y	Z

```
__ __ __ __    __    __ __ __ ,    __    __ __ __ __    __ __    __ __ __
18  3  23 10   22    17 22 23      22    18  8 10 26    26  4    17 22 23


__ __ __ __    __ __    __ __ __ __ __ __ __ __ __ __ __    __ __ __
11 22  5 23    12  7     9 19  8 10 17 14  8 26  3 23 19    18  3  4


__ __ __ __    __ __ __ __ __ __ __ __ __    __ __    __ __ __
17 22 23 17    13 23  8 15 23 14 20 11 11  7    22 10     3 22 16


__ __ __ __ __ ,    __ __ __    __ __ __ __ __ __ __ __ __    __ __ __ __
16 11 23 23 13      10  4 26    16 15 19 23  8 12 22 10  9    11 22  5 23


__ __ __    __ __ __    __ __ __ __ __ __ __ __ __    __ __    __ __ __
 8 11 11    26  3 23    13  8 16 16 23 10  9 23 19 16    22 10     3 22 16


__ __ __ .
15  8 19
```

```
by __ __ __ __    __ __ __ __ __ __
   18 22 11 11    19  4  9 23 19 16
```

ESCAPE
THE PAGE

Can you find the five pairs of keys that are the same shape but different colors? Once you do, use the number on the leftmost of the pair, top to bottom, as your exit code.

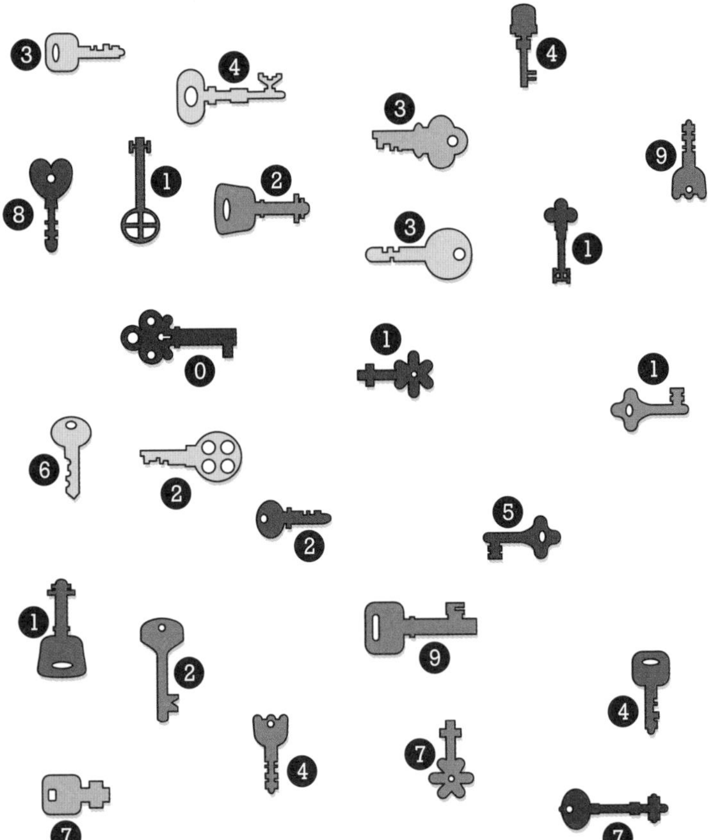

EXIT CODE

LOGIC
PUZZLE

Here is a super-tough logic puzzle. A mineral vendor sells stones at a rock and gem show. The stones peddled are: opal, pearl, quartz, ruby, sapphire, topaz, uranium, and viridine. Each has an unusual color: aqua, blue, cream, dandelion, ecru, fuchsia, green, and honey. The vendor labeled each one with a number to keep track of the stock, numbers 1–8. Unfortunately, the paperwork was soaked in the rain and the vendor can only see some of the labeling. Using what is still legible, can you figure out which color and number matches each mineral? You might want to set up a grid for this one!

1 Topaz isn't ecru, fuchsia, green, or honey-colored.
2 The uranium is blue and the quartz is green.
3 Dandelion was labeled number 3 and the viridine was labeled number 4.
4 The label number 5 wasn't on the aqua, blue, or cream stone or on the opal, pearl, or quartz.
5 The pearl is cream-colored.
6 The blue mineral isn't even numbered.
7 The sapphire is number 7.
8 The green stone isn't odd numbered.
9 The ruby is odd and the number is greater than 3.
10 The topaz isn't aqua.
11 The ecru and honey stones are greater than 5.
12 The green stone is number 2.
13 The aqua mineral is numbered something smaller than the fuchsia.
14 The pearl is number 6.
15 The honey mineral is the highest number.

1 ....
2 ....
3 ....
4 ....
5 ....
6 ....
7 ....
8 ....

FLOWERS
CRYPTOGRAM

This is a simple substitution cryptogram using pictures. The answer is a quote by a famous person. Think about what letters can possibly follow an apostrophe and what word might start a question. The letter "E" has been placed for you to get you started.

__ __ __   __ __ __ __ '__ __ __ __ E

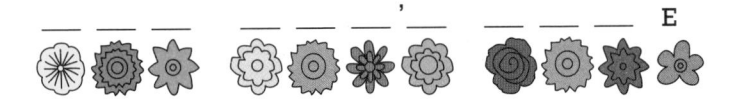

E __ E __ __ __ __ __ __ __ __ __ .   __ __ E __ E

__ __ __ __ __   __ __ __   __ __ __   __ __?

by   __ __ E __ E __   __ __ __ __ __ __ __

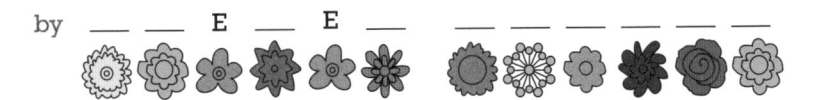

MEDIUM

BRITISH-STYLE
QUICK CROSSWORD

ACROSS

1 Object at the center of St. Peter's Square (7)
5 Touch or taste (5)
8 Feeling (7)
9 Public persona (5)
10 Bombay or Tanqueray (3)
11 Impoverished (5)
14 Out of bed (5)
15 Profound attitude reversal (6, 2, 5)
20 Kind of tropical nut (5)
21 Panache (5)
24 Zodiac sign of summer (3)
25 Many a Bob Marley fan (5)
26 Combat clothing (7)
27 Doctrine (5)
28 *The Wizard of Oz* disaster (7)

DOWN

1 Neptune's domain (5)
2 Marry secretly (5)
3 Coldly (5)
4 Where a fair trial is impossible (8, 5)
5 Popeye's favorite veggie (7)
6 Falls on the Canada/US border (7)
7 Tin or hydrogen (7)
12 Biblical ending to giv- or tak-
13 Hubbub (3)
15 Bob Fosse Oscar winner from 1972 (7)
16 Craftsman (7)
17 Intrepid (6)
18 Building wing (3)
19 French king (30)
21 Tuck, for one (5)
22 Hello in Hilo (5)
23 Juliet's love (5)

SMART TIP

Next time you're making a list, try using your non-dominant hand to write it. Using your left hand if you're right-handed (or vice versa) challenges your brain to work in a new way. This gives it a great workout and, if you stick with it, it's rewarding to see just how much you can improve. You could even try filling in this puzzle using your non-dominant hand for fun!

SILLY
BILLY

What would happen if the person who named the walkie-talkie renamed common items? See if you can match up the wacky new names on the left to the items on the right.

FUNNY MONEY ●   ● CAT

FURRY PURRY ●   ● COMEDIAN'S PAY

HEARTY STARTY ●   ● DEFIBRILLATOR

HEATIE FEETIES ●   ● FORK

LICKIE STICKIE ●   ● GLASSES CASE

MAYBE BABY ●   ● NIGHTMARE

PEEPER KEEPER ●   ● PARROT

QUICKIE STICKIE ●   ● PREGNANCY TEST

SCOOPY SOUPY ●   ● SOCKS

SCREAMY DREAMY ●   ● SPOON

STABBY GRABBY ●   ● STAMP

WORDIE BIRDIE ●   ● SUPERGLUE

HIDDEN
BRIDGES

Search for hidden words in the following sentences. Hint: All the words have four letters and belong in the same category. The hidden words will always bridge between at least two words.

When Smeagol didn't have the ring, he was more like a hobbit.

Mr. Darcy announced that he didn't care for the music at the country dance.

Don't drop a load of bricks on my flowerbed!

The ninja detached the weapons from their bearers with ease.

The football hero announced his retirement after he won the big game.

I ate almost half of the extra-large pizza myself.

The mattress began to sag everywhere. It was very uncomfortable.

As a chorus trilled their way through a hymn, I fell asleep.

Don't rub your nose at dinner.

Knowledge is like underwear. It is useful to have it, but not necessary to show it off.

—Bill Murray

SCRAMBLE
ANAGRAMS

In these two puzzles, you need to unscramble the letters within the words. Then, rearrange the highlighted letters to form the mystery word that completes the quip.

FRADT   _ _ _ _ _

ADLAS   _ _ _ _ _

DANLB   _ _ _ _ _

OTAIR   _ _ _ _ _

MLBUA   _ _ _ _ _

_ _ _ _ _: a word boring people use to describe fun people.
—*Jenny Mollen*

OSSAL   _ _ _ _ _

AANER   _ _ _ _ _

TTEEN   _ _ _ _ _

TTEEH   _ _ _ _ _

SSPER   _ _ _ _ _

I can still remember a time when I knew more than my _ _ _ _ _.
—*Clarke Kant*

CANDY
LOGIC PUZZLE

Here are two logic puzzles. Use logic to pick out which candy is being referred to by the following clues:

CANDY 1
1 The candy is one color.
2 The candy has at least some pink.
3 The candy isn't round.

CANDY 2
1 The candy is more than one color.
2 The candy isn't pink.
3 The candy isn't round.
4 The candy has at least some orange.
5 The candy is striped.

TOUGH
CRYPTOGRAMS

Here are two substitution cryptograms using letters. Each answer is a quote by a famous person.

A	B	C	D	E	F	G	H	I	J	K	L	M	N	O	P	Q	R	S	T	U	V	W	X	Y	Z

_ _ _ _ _ _   _ _ _ _ _ _   _ _ _ _   _ _ _ _ _ _ ,
U A Y U H T   C L J E W Z N   H L P J   N R N I W N T

_ _ _ _ _ _ _   _ _ _ _ _ _   _ _ _ _   _ _   _ _ _ _ .
R L G X W R E   U R R L H T   G X N I   T L   I P D X

by _ _ _ _ _   _ _ _ _ _
   L T D U J   Y W A F N

A	B	C	D	E	F	G	H	I	J	K	L	M	N	O	P	Q	R	S	T	U	V	W	X	Y	Z

_ _ _   _ _ _   _ _ _   _ _ _ _ _   _ _ _ _ _ _
G O O   N R H   G U R   R Z A G O   S R I C U R

_ _ _ _ .
I Q Y T

by _ _ _ _ _ _ _   _ _ _ _ _ _
   T R U S R U V   T C C L R U

ESCAPE
THE PAGE

Seeing double? Each word in the grid is missing a doubled letter. The definitions for the words are below the grid, but in random order. Can you match the definitions and fill in the blanks? When you're done, you'll have to search to find your exit code.

	F	A		E	N	
G	L	O		O	R	M
	B	R		C	H	
C	H	I		I	E	R
	R	E		E	D	
C	A	R		R	E	D

Not so warm

Gunned, as an engine

Luminous larvae

Make plump

Rushed wildly

Feet-first birth

EXIT CODE

QUOTE
FALL

To solve this puzzle, choose a letter from each column and drop it straight down into the grid below. Since there is more than one letter per column, the trick is to figure out where the letters should go. The black squares are spaces and a word can wrap around to the next row. When you're done, you'll end up with a quote by Steven Wright.

E		E	I		E				
I		I	N		E	N	D	D	A
O		L	O	T	G	O	F	F	R
R	V	S	R	V	S	O	O	O	T
	■							■	
	■					■			
				■			■		
	■			■					■

SMART TIP

Exercise can improve your memory. Research has shown that even low-intensity exercise is associated with increased activity in the hippocampus, the part of the brain that deals with learning. So, give your brain a boost and go for a walk.

FAMOUS MOVIE
SONGS QUIZ

You must remember this... song. Can you figure out which song goes with which movie? For a tougher challenge, cover up the bottom of the page and see if you can name a tune from each.

1 *Pinocchio* ....

2 *Dirty Dancing* ....

3 *The Lion King* ....

4 *The Graduate* ....

5 *Titanic* ....

6 *Breakfast at Tiffany's* ....

7 *Saturday Night Fever* ....

8 *Wizard of Oz* ....

9 *Top Hat* ....

10 *Casablanca* ....

As Time Goes By
Can You Feel the Love Tonight?
Cheek to Cheek
(I've Had) The Time of My Life
Moon River

Mrs. Robinson
My Heart Will Go On
Over the Rainbow
Stayin' Alive
When You Wish Upon a Star

UNKNOWABLE
NUMBERS: FOOD AND DRINK

Can you answer the following questions about food and drink? When you've finished, the letters associated with the answers will create a word.

1 How many liters of alcohol is drunk per person per year in Moldova?
d 5   e 9   f 13   g 17

2 Almonds, one of the most nutritious foods, contain how much magnesium in a 2oz (60g) serving?
a 150mg   b 1,500mg   c 15mg   d 1.5mg

3 How many million tons of salmon were farmed globally in 2018?
q 1.1   r 4.4   s 2.2   t 3.3

4 Italy is the world's top producer of wine. How many million hectoliters did Italy make in 2019?
t 47.5   u 66.5   v 78.5   w 86.5

5 The world's most popular cookie is Oreo. What were Oreo sales in 2019?
p US$1 billion   q US$2 billion   r US$3 billion   s US$4 billion

6 How long ago were cattle first domesticated?
o 10,000 years   p 50,000 years   q 25,000 years   r 5,000 years

7 What year was the Caesar salad invented?
k 1914   l 1944   m 1934   n 1924

8 How many cups of flour are in a pound?
n 3   o 4   p 7   q 8

9 In billion kilograms, how much cows' milk does the United States produce?
m 91.3   n 44.6   o 78.2   p 63.6

10 How many 1oz shots are there in a liter bottle of alcohol?
w 14   x 51   y 22   z 126

ANSWER ....

JAPANESE
ETYMOLOGY

Japanese is an interesting language. It has a special phonetic alphabet, *katakana*, for words brought in from other languages. These sounds are used as exactly as possible, but Japanese language always puts a vowel between consonant sounds. These particular words always end in a vowel, regardless of whether the English words do. Can you sound out and identify the English words?

ア	エ	イ	ン
a	e	i	so
ウ	カ	ケ	キ
u	ka	ke	ki
コ	ク	パ	テ
ko	ku	pa	te
ピ	ラ	プ	ナ
pi	ra	pu	na
メ	チ	ト	ツ
me	chi	to	tsu
タ	ユ	ジ	ロ
ta	yu	ji	ro
ヌ	—	ワ	リ
nu	long vowel	wa	ri
ド	ス	チャ	オ
do	su	cha	o

ENGLISH WORDS

America
Computer
Crossword
Jet ski
Ketchup
Laptop
Pantsuit

Party
Password
Patchwork
Peanuts
Text
Vodka
Whiskey

JAPANESE WORDS

パスワード ....

ジェットスキー ....

ラップトップ ....

クロスワード ....

パーティー ....

アメリカ ....

ピーナッツ ....

ケチャップ ....

パッチワーク ....

ウィスキー ....

コンピュータ ....

パンツスーツ ....

ウォッカ ....

テキスト ....

EASY

NUMBERS
LOGIC

Can you figure out which number matches which letter in this easy logic puzzle?

$E \times E = I = E + E$ ....

$EE - E = EN = I \times M$ ....

$ME \div E = EA$ ....

$AM \div M = DC = A + L$ ....

$C \times C = U = D + R$ ....

1	2	3	4	5	6	7	8	9	0

SMART TIP

Something as simple as a cup of coffee may help to improve your memory. Caffeine makes you more alert, which can improve memory and concentration. But be careful not to drink too much or have a cup in the evening, as this can have a negative impact on sleep quality, which over time can cause a decline in memory and concentration.

TEXT
TWIST

You can actually understand more of script than you'd think with just a little bit of a word showing. Do your best to decipher this message, even with more than half of the words covered up.

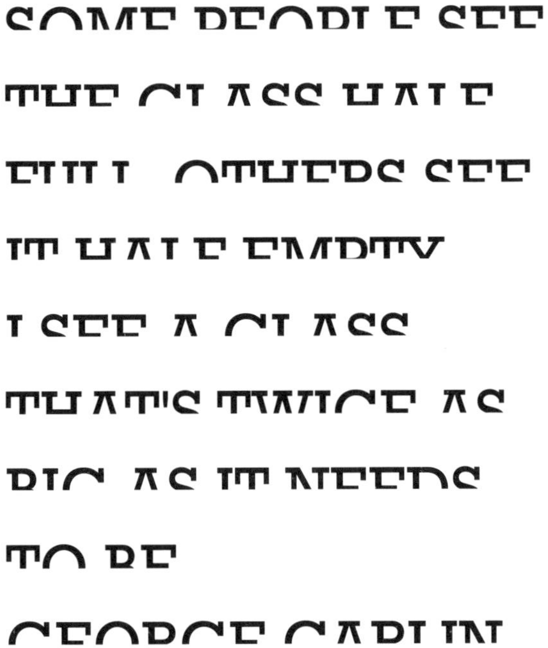

SOME PEOPLE SEE

THE GLASS HALF

FULL. OTHERS SEE

IT HALF EMPTY.

I SEE A GLASS

THAT'S TWICE AS

BIG AS IT NEEDS

TO BE.

GEORGE CARLIN

SUDOKU

Can you fill in the blanks of the grid with the numbers 1–9? Make sure that no number repeats in any row, column, or within a 3 x 3 area.

1			4			5	8	
5	9	8					3	7
7	6				8			
				1	3		6	
9						2		
						7	9	1
		1		4				
		9		2	6			
		6	8	9	1			4

If you are curious, you'll find the puzzles around you. If you are determined, you will solve them.

—Erno Rubik

CIRCULAR
FILL IN THE BLANKS

To solve these six puzzles, add a letter to the blank space in each circle to make a six-letter word. You'll have to figure out whether the word is winding around in a clockwise or counterclockwise direction. And you'll have to decide where the word starts within the circle. To aid in solving, the letters that you fill in will also spell a six-letter word.

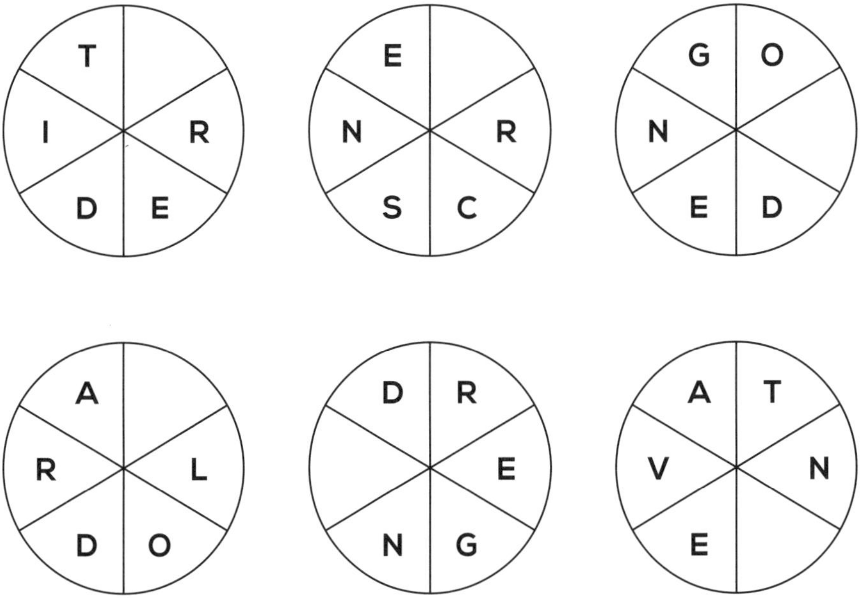

Puzzle 1: T, I, R, D, E

Puzzle 2: E, N, R, S, C

Puzzle 3: G, O, N, E, D

Puzzle 4: A, R, L, D, O

Puzzle 5: D, R, E, N, G

Puzzle 6: A, T, V, N, E

SIX-LETTER WORD ....

FAMOUS PETS
QUIZ

1 At a US president's funeral, his wicked pet parrot swore so much that he had to be carried out of the house. Which president was it?
a Andrew Jackson   **b** Woodrow Wilson   **c** Abraham Lincoln   **d** John Adams

2 The Marquis de Lafayette was gifted an alligator on his travels around the US He re-gifted the alligator to the president at the time. Who was it?
a Abraham Lincoln   **b** Bill Clinton   **c** George Bush   **d** John Quincy Adams

3 Queen Victoria's Pekingese dog was one of the first to come to the UK from China. What was her dog's name?
a Francis   **b** Looty   **c** Josephine   **d** Macbeth

4 What was the name of President Nixon's cocker spaniel, who is said to have saved his political career?
a Daisy   **b** Socks   **c** Max   **d** Checkers

5 Who owned Bubbles the chimpanzee?
a TS Eliot   **b** George Bush   **c** Queen Elizabeth II   **d** Michael Jackson

6 Charles Dickens loved his cat so much that when the cat passed away, he had its paw turned into a letter opener. What was the special cat's name?
a Bob   **b** Fluffy   **c** Maggie   **d** Whiskers

7 Josephine Baker had an exotic pet, Chiquita, that performed with her, lived with her, and even slept in her bed. What kind of animal was it?
a Porcupine   **b** Wolf   **c** Cheetah   **d** Raccoon

8 Nicolas Cage has spent a reported US$150,000 on one of these sea creatures. What is it?
a Octopus   **b** Goldfish   **c** Lobster   **d** Nautilus

9 Alexander the Great had a horse that he really loved, even going to the length of naming a city after it. The horse's name means 'ox head' in Greek. What was it?
a Boveletus   **b** Buster   **c** Bucephalus   **d** Bovetete

10 Which eccentric artist had an ocelot named Babou?
a Escher   **b** Picasso   **c** Warhol   **d** Dali

QUOTE
FALL

To solve this puzzle, choose a letter from each column and drop it straight down into the grid below. Since there is more than one letter per column, the trick is to figure out where the letters should go. The black squares are spaces and a word can wrap around to the next row. When you're done, you'll end up with a quote by George Burns.

	D									
G	E		D		G	A		E		
I	F	E	A	D		A	L	E	A	E
N	L	H	B	E	I	E	M	E	D	E
P	O	R	E	I	F	E	N	I	P	E	O
T	O	R	Y	O	T	O	O	P	V	H	T
V	T	T	Y	T	U	Y	W	U	V	S	U

CAT
SUDOKU

Can you fill in the blanks of the grid with each cat image? Make sure that no cat repeats in any row, column, or within a 3 x 3 area. You could assign each cat a number to make solving easier.

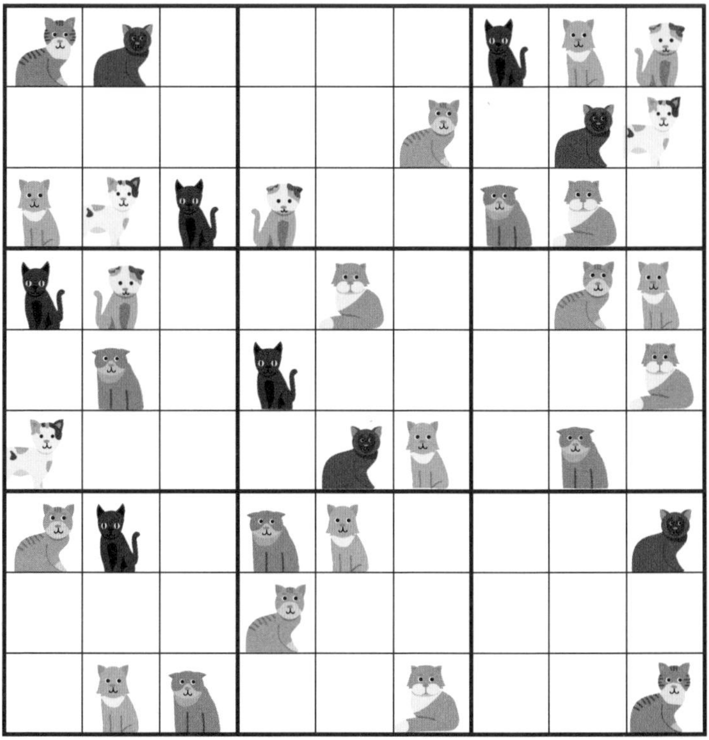

SCRAMBLE
ANAGRAMS

Unscramble the letters within the words in these two sets of anagrams. Then, rearrange the highlighted letters to form the mystery word that completes the quip.

RACZ   __ __ __ __

AALS   __ __ __ __

BEOY   __ __ __ __

LPOA   __ __ __ __

I won't be shaving this November in order to raise awareness for how
__ __ __ __ I am.
—*Tim Siedell*

EEBT   __ __ __ __

OBLB   __ __ __ __

ALLT   __ __ __ __

CHEO   __ __ __ __

What did the zero say to the eight? Nice __ __ __ __.

TRIVIA
MATCHING

Starting at the top of the left-hand column and working your way down, match the countries to their capitals by drawing a line to join the dots next to each name. When you're done, read the letters you've crossed, in the order you crossed them, to find a phrase.

ERITREA •   T   H   B   • TRIPOLI

CHINA •   V   E   R   U   E   T   • VALLETTA

JORDAN •   A   O   G   J   A R   V   • ASMARA

EAST TIMOR •   C   R   B   O   A   A   C   • HAGATNA

GUAM •   I   T   E   P   • DILI

ESTONIA •   L   M   T   B N Q   A   • TALLINN

LIBYA •   S   D   I   Q   L   O   • BEIJING

MALTA •   T U   Y   U   R   • SUVA

NEW ZEALAND •   W   G O   N   E   • AMMAN

FIJI •   H F   I   I   X E K   N   T   • WELLINGTON

ANSWER ....

We don't stop playing because we grow old —we grow old because we stop playing.

—George Bernard Shaw

BRITISH-STYLE
QUICK CROSSWORD

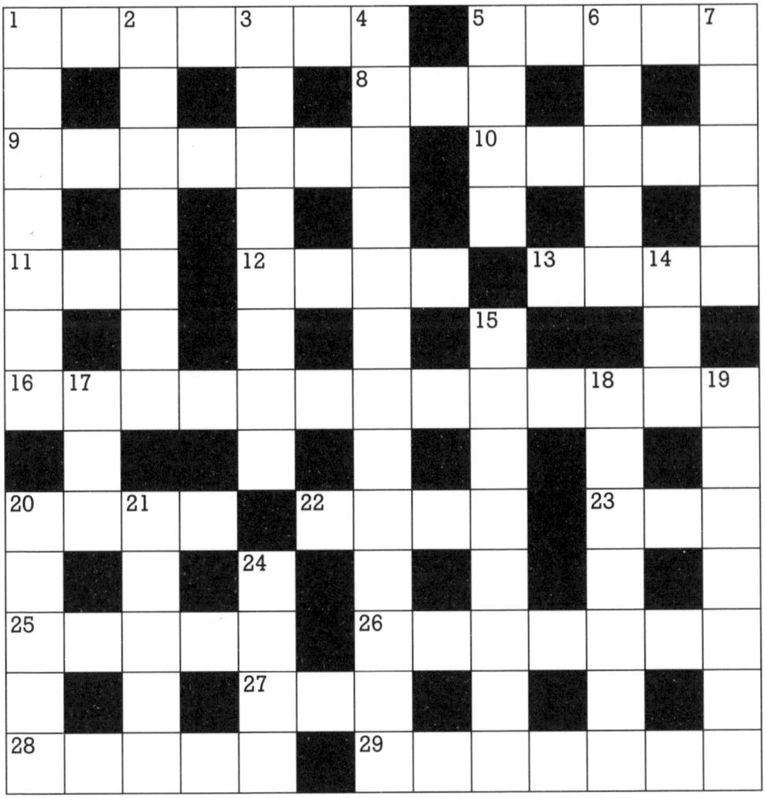

ACROSS

1 Egyptian tourist attraction (7)
5 Representative (5)
8 Groove (3)
9 Regret (7)
10 Poppy product (5)
11 Turner who started CNN
12 *Casablanca* female lead (4)
13 Calendar unit (4)
16 Sprinkled with gray, as hair (4, 3, 6)
20 Footwear (4)
22 Facial feature (4)
23 Zilch (3)
25 Vision (5)
26 Dazzle (7)
27 Snaky fish (3)
28 Brother's daughter (5)
29 Portable lamp (7)

DOWN

1 Jolly Roger fliers (7)
2 Renovate (7)
3 Almond paste icing (8)
4 Wearing drop-dead gorgeous clothes (7, 2, 4)
5 Tiny particle (4)
6 Top-notch (5)
7 Lion trainer (5)
14 High card (3)
15 Leader of *The Lost Boys*, who fights with 1-Down (5, 3)
17 Volcanic output (3)
18 Conjunctivitis (7)
19 Accumulates rapidly, as in fog (5, 2)
20 Typical 4-door car or historical chair (5)
21 Plump (5)
24 Captain Hook's sidekick, enemy of 15-Down (4)

SMART TIP

If you want to exercise lots of your brain, then grab some yarn and needles and get knitting. Following the pattern activates the frontal lobe responsible for attention and processing; watching where the needles and yarn go uses the occipital lobe, which processes visual information; and making the stitches uses the parietal lobe, which deals with spatial navigation and sensory information. With your brain working in all these areas, knitting is the perfect activity for helping to keep your mind sharp—as well as producing woolly wonders to keep you warm!

SOCCER
CRISSCROSS

Fit the soccer, or football, words into the grid.

BICYCLE KICK	INDIRECT FREE KICK	RED CARD
BRACE	NUTMEG	SLIDING TACKLE
CLEAR	OBSTRUCTION	STRIKER
DRIBBLE	OFFSIDE	SWEEPER
DROP KICK	ONE TOUCH	THROW IN
EXTRA TIME	OPEN GOAL	TRAP
FIRST TOUCH	OWN GOAL	VANISHING SPRAY
FREE KICK	PANENKA	WORLD CUP
GOAL KICK	PENALTY	ZONE DEFENSE
GOALKEEPER	REBOUND	

ESCAPE
THE PAGE

Are you good at following directions? Start with the common phrase "test one's mettle" and, step by step, modify it. When you're done, you'll have your exit code.

T	E	S	T	O	N	E	S	M	E	T	T	L	E

1 Change the 3rd letter to the letter before it in the alphabet.

....

2 Change any L to V.

....

3 If there are 4 Ts, change the 3rd one to F.

....

4 Change the 9th letter to the letter after it in the alphabet.

....

5 Change the 5th and 12th letters to I.

....

6 Change the 4th and 8th letters to O.

....

7 Add an N after the 4th letter.

....

8 The 1st letter changes to the last letter in the alphabet.

....

EXIT CODE

MAZE

Enter the maze at "In" and find the correct path to "Out" as quickly as you can.

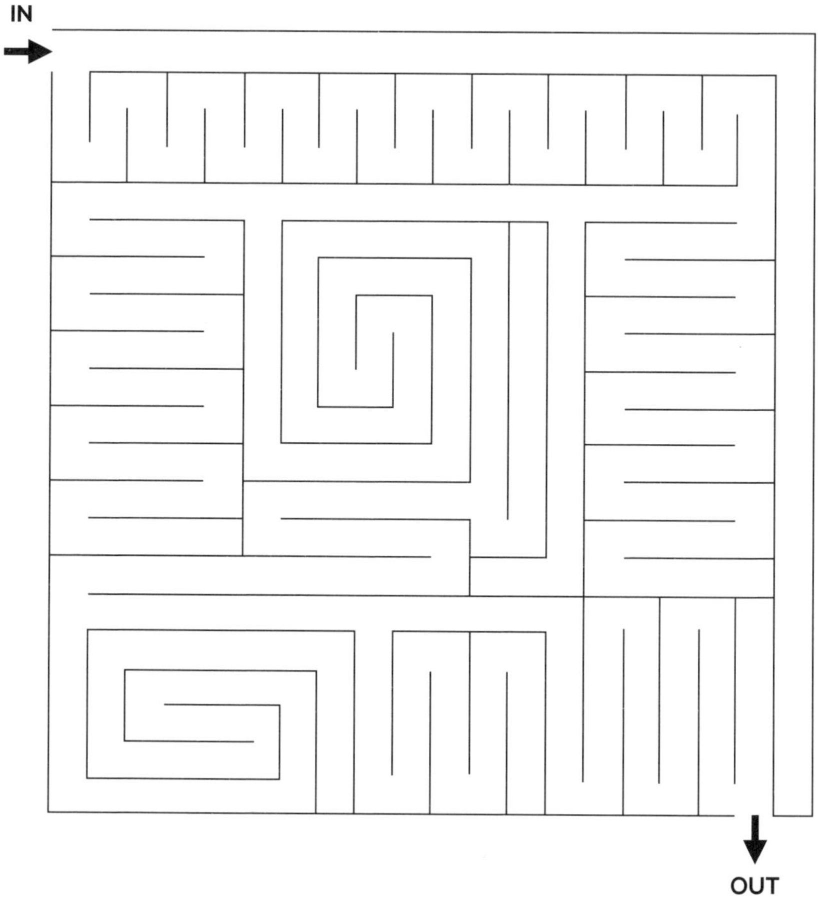

IN

OUT

ADD A LETTER
TO A MOVIE TITLE

Adding a letter to a movie title allows us to reimagine the plot of the movie. Can you match the funny plot change to the original movies listed at the bottom of the page? For example, the plot "an unlikely trio search for wigs" could be matched to THE GOOD, THE BAD AND THE UGLY to make THE GOOD, THE BALD AND THE UGLY.

1 In the capable hands of Pixar, *The Iliad* is reimagined from the wooden horse's point of view.

2 This comedy centers on a future bride who is trying to slim down in time for her wedding.

3 A sad tale about a guy who can never get other guys to call him by his shortened name: they always just call him "Ronald."

4 In this sci-fi thriller, our heroes have landed on a new world that is dominated by slithering reptiles.

5 Here's another thrilling adaptation of *Death of a Salesman*, but there's a twist: the protagonist does nothing but huff and puff.

6 A girl tries to call attention to saving the planet by brightly coloring her teeth. It doesn't catch on as a fashion statement.

7 In this dystopian future, corn is illegal. A renegade fills up his backpack and trots his way through all checkpoints to get to the city. Nachos for everyone!

8 Bored kids trapped inside because of bad weather are competing to see who can get to the top step first. Will someone take a tumble?

9 A man inherits a members-only haunted house operation. The first rule of running it? You don't talk about it.

10 In old Hollywood, a trio discovers that the storm sewers make your voice sound amazing!

ANT MAN
DIE HARD
FIGHT CLUB
THE GREEN MILE
IRON MAN
THE MAZE RUNNER
SINGIN' IN THE RAIN
SNAKES ON A PLANE
STAR WARS
TOY STORY

CIRCULAR
FILL IN THE BLANKS

To solve these puzzles, add a letter to the blank space in each circle to make a seven-letter word. You'll have to figure out whether the word is winding around in a clockwise or counterclockwise direction. And you'll have to decide where the word starts within the circle. To aid in solving, the letters that you fill in will spell a six-letter word.

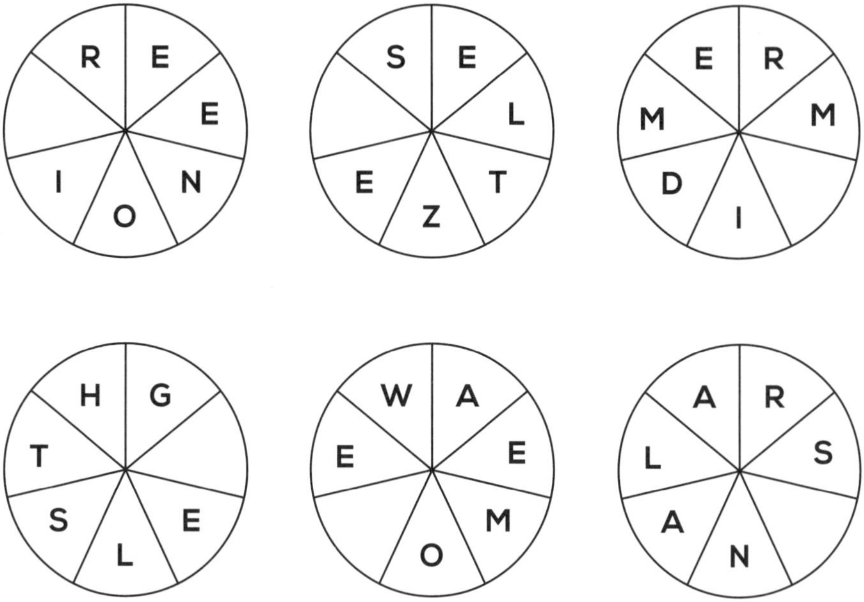

Circle 1: R, E, E, N, O, I

Circle 2: S, E, L, T, Z, E

Circle 3: E, R, M, M, I, D

Circle 4: H, G, E, L, S, T

Circle 5: W, A, E, M, O, E

Circle 6: A, R, S, N, A, L

SIX-LETTER WORD ....

SCRAMBLE
ANAGRAMS

Unscramble the letters within the words below. Then, rearrange the highlighted letters to form the mystery word that completes the quip.

TES   _ _ _

NOI   _ _ _

ETO   _ _ _

If I were two-faced, would I be wearing this _ _ _ ?
—*Abraham Lincoln*

SMART TIP

Next time you find yourself reaching for a calculator to work something out, why not grab a piece of paper and a pencil instead? Exercising your skills with numbers is an excellent challenge and you can always check your answer using the calculator later. If you're feeling brave, see if you can work the sum out in your head!

CATEGORY
CROSSOUTS

In each grid below, you can take the letters from a square in each column, reading left to right, to make a word. All of the words in a grid belong to the same category. Feel free to cross out the letters, as each square will be used only once. It's up to you to figure out which category goes with which grid.

AS	A	E	LE
M	P	UC	E
WA	PR	P	T
S	L	NU	N

....
....
....
....

S	R	OU	N
MA	AL	O	T
T	CH	L	VY
AN	ER	C	IN
P	R	MO	H

....
....
....
....
....

OR	ZA	LI	IA
A	C	LE	P
T	O	N	D
BE	U	HI	S
CR	GO	CU	A

....
....
....
....
....

FISH   FLOWERS   TREES

The mind, once stretched by a new idea, never returns to its original dimensions.

—Ralph Waldo Emerson

PRIMARIES
CROSSWORD

Take a look at the title of this crossword and see if you can guess what topic links the longest entries—the theme answers.

ACROSS

1 Warning device
6 Biblical prophet
10 Chimps, gorillas, or orangutans
14 *Andrea* _____ (ill-fated ship)
15 Fat-removal procedure, for short
16 "To _____ and to hold"
17 Nike rival with gel shoes
18 Biblical garden
19 Suit to _____ (2 words)
20 Misleading clues
23 Finish
24 Rodent
25 24-Across and roaches, for example
27 _____ column
31 Pacific or Atlantic
34 *Water Lilies* painter Claude
35 Urban transport on rails
36 "And to _____ good night!" (2 words)
40 Extremely rarely (5 words)
43 Neuter, as a horse
44 Leaf's angle
45 TV, newspapers, and radio
46 _____ on thick: exaggerate (2 words)
48 Kind of old movie
49 Pale
52 Massachusetts airport, abbr.
53 President after GWB
54 The world's first national park
62 Penny _____
64 French sky
65 Leafy retreat
66 Beginning of a Cockney toast
67 Follow, as advice
68 Queen, in Spain

69 HA and Margret, who created *Curious George*
70 Yours and mine
71 Himalayan Sasquatches

DOWN

1 Jewish month before Nisan
2 Mislay
3 Dry
4 Luxurious
5 Italian competitor of Ferrari
6 Something 1-Across does
7 Calf-length skirt
8 Door sign
9 Melody
10 "I see!"
11 Tops of heads
12 There are 10 in a decathlon
13 Bird feeder supply
21 *Too-Ra-Loo-Ra-Loo-_____* Irish lullaby
22 Relaxing resort
26 Tooth covering
27 Urban air pollution
28 Cornmeal cake
29 Contain: abbr.
30 Seattle sight: Space _____
31 Planet's path
32 Phone
33 Ostrich's cousin
35 Yellow or black cab
37 Miner's pay dirt
38 Pork cut
39 Med. school subject (for short)
41 Dissenting vote

42 Ambassador, e.g.
47 Some
48 Scatter, as 13-Down
49 More fit
50 Be generous
51 Sweet bee product
52 Emphasizes a font
55 Reverberate
56 In _____ of (as a replacement for)
57 Ogle
58 You'll find one in 65-Across
59 RIP notice

60 Anika _____ Rose, Tony winner for *A Raisin in the Sun*
61 Historical times
63 Ending for baron or viscount

ONE-LETTER
CHANGE

Change one letter of each word below to make the name of a country. For example, if you change the R in GRAM to a U, you'll get GUAM.

PERK	....	LASS	....
MALT	....	TUBA	....
OMEN	....	BRAN	....
CHAP	....	LIBRA	....
TIGER	....	WHILE	....
CHINE	....	STAIN	....
MANTA	....	SEPAL	....
TATAR	....	BEGIN	....
TONYA	....	ROLAND	....
ANGORA	....	TRANCE	....

ESCAPE
THE PAGE

Can you find the subject and hidden words in the grid? The shape of the word search is a hint. When you're done, you'll have to search to find your exit code.

```
            F  O  P  U
         R  T  L  E  V  E
      N  J  U  P  I  T  E  R
   N  I  T  S  N  E  T  E  N  E
   N  O  M  E  R  C  U  R  Y  U
I  M  E  T  S  Y  S  R  A  L  O  S  S  S  Y
   O  U  A  R  O  R  M  B  U  I
   E  N  U  T  P  E  N  N  T  A
      L  E  X  U  I  A  T  C
         O  E  A  R  T  H
         D  U  E  N
```

EXIT CODE

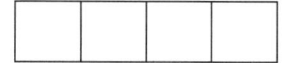

HIDDEN
MESSAGE ....

SAME LETTER
START "S"

Answer as many of these five-letter words that begin with "S" as you can. For an extra challenge, give yourself a time limit. When you're done, read down the highlighted diagonal for another five-letter "S" word.

Typical 4-door car or historical chair

Grin

Theater platform

Sleeper's sound

Sugary

"S" WORD ....

SMART TIP

Puzzles are perfect for giving your brain a workout, but if you fancy doing something you can share with friends and family, try card games. There are hundreds of different games and they are all great for developing your problem-solving skills and decision making. They are also a great excuse for getting together with others and having fun.

PICTURE
FILL IN THE BLANKS

Name the toys in the pictures, then fit them into the blanks in the words below.
How many can you complete?

 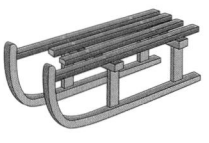 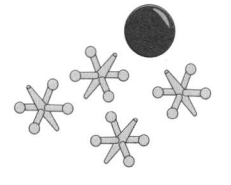 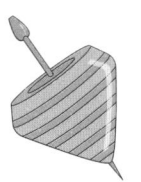

RES _ _ _ _ _ ED   _ _ _ _ ERINA

_ _ _ _ OP   S _ _ _ LET

AU _ _ _ SY   _ _ _ _ _ ADE

LUMBER _ _ _ _ _   TOU _ _ _ _

HIDDEN
BRIDGES

Search for hidden words in the following sentences. Hint: All the words are 3–5 letters and belong in the same category. The hidden words will always bridge between at least two words.

The hairpin estate roads made me carsick. ....

If I have to row another boat, these blisters will pop! ....

Help me set up this easel, my dear, the light is perfect. ....

The opera's penultimate aria was transporting. ....

Could it be echoes that we're hearing? ....

Get out the big umbrella, it's raining cats and dogs. ....

Let me show you a brief I read yesterday. ....

I ate a kiwi that was really sour. ....

When I went to Nepal, my days were full of hikes and photographing the majestic Himalayas. ....

The emerald Erie waters sparkled and danced in the sun. ....

SCRAMBLE
ANAGRAMS

Unscramble the letters within the words below. Then, rearrange the highlighted letters to form the mystery word that completes the quip.

DER   __ __ __

SEY   __ __ __

UCE   __ __ __

YRT   __ __ __

__ __ __ __: the word computer professionals use when they mean "idiot."
—*Dave Berry*

TUO   __ __ __

TTO   __ __ __

RON   __ __ __

XAE   __ __ __

I quit my job at the helium gas factory. I refuse to be spoken to in that __ __ __ __ .
—*Stewart Francis*

LOGIC
PUZZLES

Use logic to work out which dog is which in these two puzzles.

....

There are four dogs. Their names are Alfie, Bowser, Carly, and Dino. Use logic to match the descriptions of the dogs to their names:

1 Alfie and Carly have ears that stand up.
2 Bowser has an orange collar.
3 Dino is between two other dogs.
4 Carly isn't black and white.

There are nine dogs. Their names are Eddie, Frasier, Greta, Hops, Inigo, Joss, Kraken, Moose, and Netta. Can you follow the clues to figure out which dog is which? Use logic to match the description of the dogs to their names:

....

1 Kraken and Frasier are the only dogs that are solely black and white.
2 Greta has a curly tail.
3 Hops and Eddie have blue collars.
4 Netta is the smallest dog.
5 Eddie, Moose, and Hops have darker ears than the rest of their coats.
6 Joss has the longest ears and Inigo has the shortest.
7 Hops has protruding teeth.
8 Frasier has an eye patch.

....

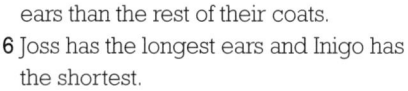

....

CATEGORY
CROSSOUTS

In each grid below, you can take the letters from a square in each column, reading left to right, to make a word. All of the words in a grid belong to the same category. Feel free to cross out the letters, as each square will be used only once. It's up to you to figure out which category goes with which grid.

EL	RI	O	LA
GO	I	HA	O
P	EP	IN	A
R	A	L	N
L	H	ND	NT

....
....
....
....
....

MU	A	C	LE
B	FF	CA	E
W	A	AG	N
SA	N	I	KE
PA	US	FF	ON

....
....
....
....
....

A	E	C	ON
B	EA	M	E
P	P	PL	H
GR	AN	P	A
L	A	AN	E

....
....
....
....
....

BREAKFAST   **FRUIT**   **ZOO**

KNOCKOUT

In the puzzle below, cross out any word that is described by the clues. When you're done, read top to bottom and left to right to get a quote by Caroline Rhea.

MATCH	MY	SUDOKU	FAVORITE	REPAID
MACHINE	TIDYING	AT	SUBTLE	THE
GYM	PAT	IS	STRETCH	THE
STATIC	VENDING	FORM	ROOK	MACHINE

CROSS OUT THE WORD THAT:

1 Is a type of puzzle.
2 Is "diaper" spelled backward.
3 Can mean "connect" or the end of a game of tennis.
4 Is "dignity" mixed up.
5 Has a silent "B."
6 Changes the meaning of the word if you add "you" after the 2nd letter.
7 Is the name of a chess piece.
8 Can come after uni- or before -ative.
9 Starts with four letters that mean "hurry!"—especially heard in a medical situation.
10 Has the pattern CCCVCCC, if C = consonant and V = vowel.

QUOTE ....

SMART TIP

Learning a new language can help to improve your brain function. There are lots of apps, courses, and languages out there, so pick one that suits you and enjoy experiencing a foreign culture without even leaving home.

TURNABOUT

Place the answer to the clue in the appropriately numbered row. Enter the answer until you run out of room, then keep going in the following row, going backward. This backward piece will be the beginning of the next answer.

Example:

The first word is POTS. The last two letters wrap around into the second row. The second word is STEP. The third word is PEER. And the fourth word is REPO, wrapping back up to the top.

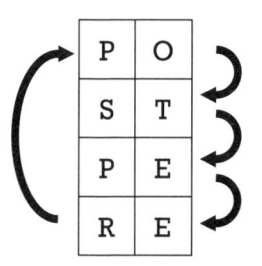

1 Stag, for one

2 Make over

3 Scent

4 Lion's warning

5 Train track

6 Maned cat

7 Lymph _ _ _ _

CONSERVATION
CROSSWORD

This tricky crossword will test your knowledge of American culture.

ACROSS

1 Crowd sound
4 Many a reggae artist
9 Stream where 18-Across are found
14 Nevada city, LYE anagram
15 Consumer information: How to avoid _____ (2 words)
16 Great Lakes natives
17 5G_____ coverage
18 Creatures studied by 65-Across
20 _____ or laurel, internet conundrum
22 Letter after kay
23 Upon
24 Place where 18-Across studied
28 Equipment
29 Coup result
34 Piece in Scrabble
37 Bank abbr.
40 Innocent
41 "Life _____" (2 words)
43 Tailless simian group that includes 18-Across
44 _____ of a coin (starting team decider) (2 words)
45 Woman's name that sounds like two letters
46 Cummerbund
48 "_____ well that ends well."
49 Go over again
51 Ogle
53 Deepest of African lakes, where 18-Across may be found
58 "Dang!"
62 Mauna _____
63 Virtual transaction

65 Subject of this puzzle: one of the "Trimates" Louis Leakey sent out to study 18-Across
69 Nibble
70 Time for lunch
71 "Long time _____!"
72 Pacific Island group or a canine sound
73 Rips up
74 Digital book, e.g.
75 Feminine suffix

DOWN

1 Depend
2 Where "I do" is said
3 Laughing dog of Africa
4 Lake Michigan city
5 Cinder
6 Biol. or Ecol.
7 More domesticated
8 Plenty
9 _____ Xer
10 Rice-like pasta
11 Countenance
12 Source of sugar
13 Fuel brand
19 Too
21 A place where 18-Across can be found
25 Air safety org.
26 Killer whales
27 Ahi
30 Drives to see animals
31 Cash drawer
32 Diabolical
33 Workout nos.
34 Level

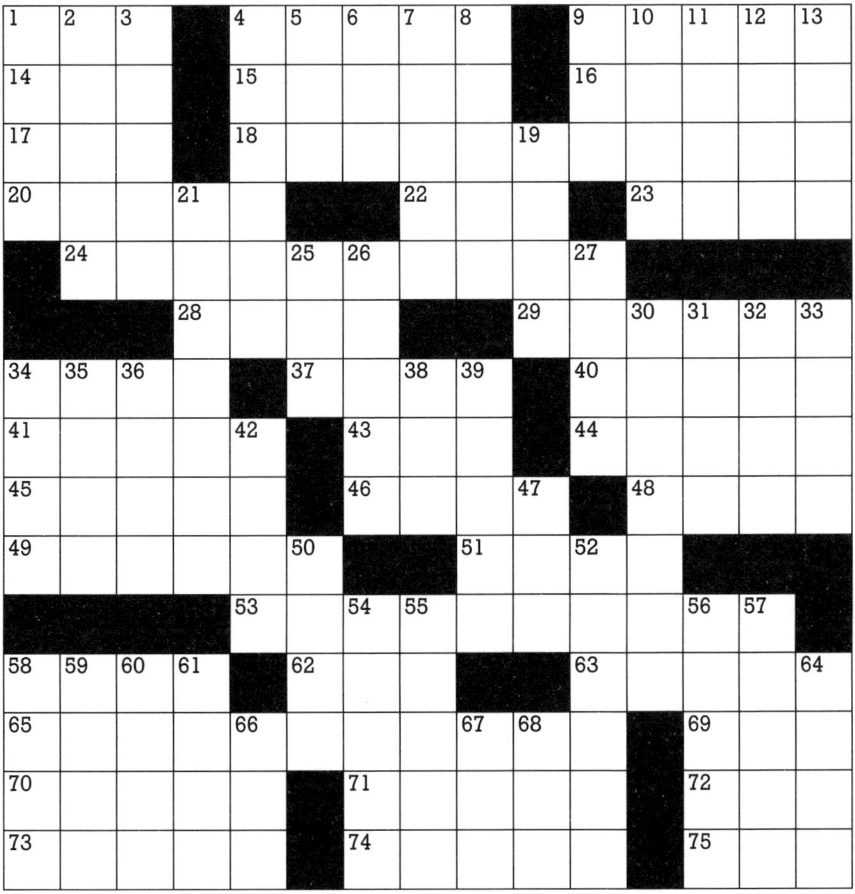

35 _____ of Capri
36 Whip
38 Tax pro
39 Inventor Nikola
42 Exam
47 Farm female
50 Angel's headgear
52 Shoelace hole
54 Nary a soul
55 Gal of *Wonder Woman*
56 Rapper West, father of North, Saint, Chicago, and Psalm

57 False name
58 Slightly open
59 Like the White Rabbit
60 Unsigned, abbr.
61 Transmit
64 Omar of *House*
66 Some TVs and appliances
67 Chemical suffix
68 Superman foe _____ Luthor

ESCAPE
THE PAGE

Answer as many of these five-letter words as you can. When you're done, read down the two highlighted columns, top to bottom, to use as your exit code.

1 Water vapor

2 Outcast

3 Meat shunner

4 Set of values

5 V-shaped mark

6 Atmospheric layer

7 Kid minder

8 Track meet piece

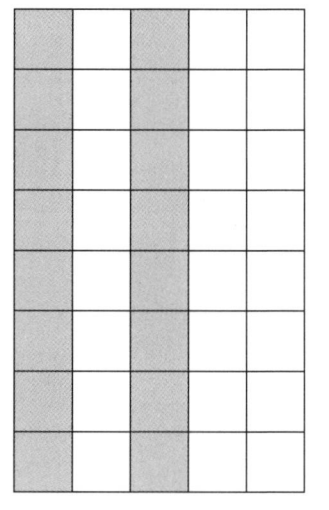

EXIT CODE

PICTURE
FILL IN THE BLANKS

Name the creatures in the pictures, then fit them into the blanks in the words below.
How many can you complete?

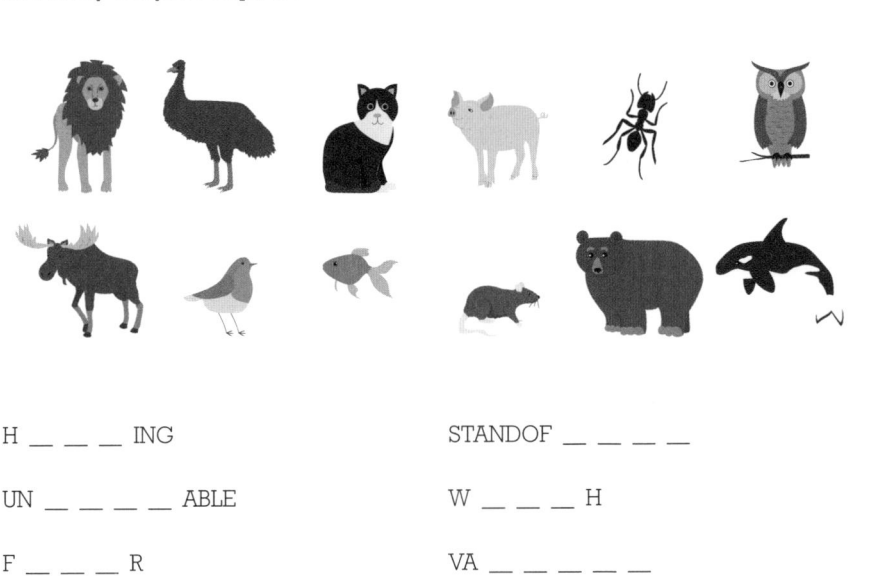

H _ _ _ ING

UN _ _ _ _ ABLE

F _ _ _ R

BIL _ _ _ _ S

MOT _ _ _ _ DE

LO _ _ _ E

STANDOF _ _ _ _

W _ _ _ H

VA _ _ _ _ _

DIS _ _ _ _ _ G

INF _ _ _ RY

E _ _ _ LOTTIS

CIRCULAR
FILL IN THE BLANKS

To solve these puzzles, add a letter to the blank space in each circle to make a seven-letter word. You'll have to figure out whether the word is winding around in a clockwise or counterclockwise direction. And you'll have to decide where the word starts within the circle. To aid in solving, the letters that you fill in will spell a six-letter word.

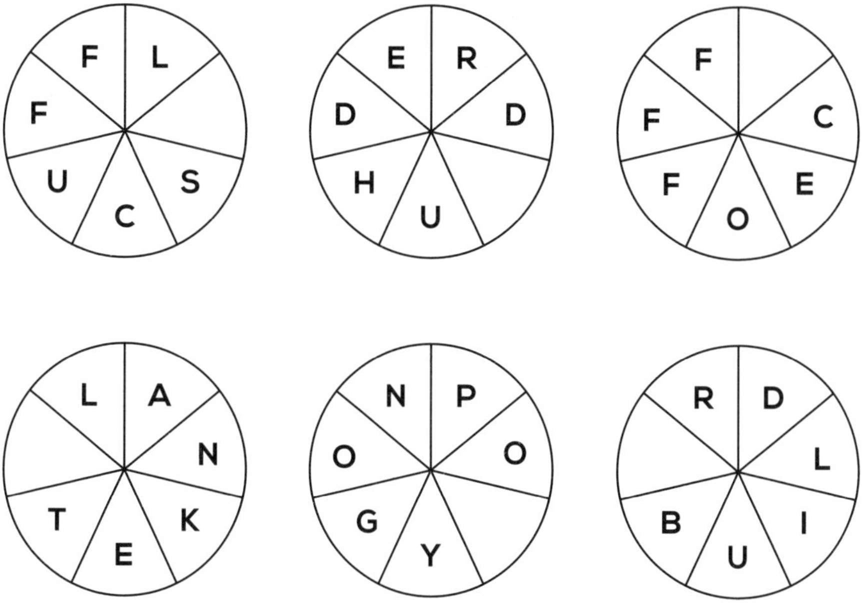

Puzzle 1: F, L, F, U, S, C

Puzzle 2: E, R, D, D, H, U

Puzzle 3: F, F, C, F, E, O

Puzzle 4: L, A, N, T, K, E

Puzzle 5: N, P, O, O, G, Y

Puzzle 6: R, D, L, B, I, U

SIX-LETTER WORD ....

OLD MOVIES
SCRAMBLE

Can you unscramble the names of the stars at the bottom of the page? They were featured in these great old movies. Can you match them up? Good luck!

1 *Singin' in the Rain* ....

2 *African Queen* ....

3 *Some Like It Hot* ....

4 *Rear Window* ....

5 *Casablanca* ....

6 *East of Eden* ....

7 *Psycho* ....

8 *The Magnificent Seven* ....

9 *Citizen Kane* ....

10 *All About Eve* ....

AMEJS NADE	KINTAAREH BUNEPHR
BEDIBE YOLNDERS	LYU NNERBYR
EANN REXBAT	OONRS LLEEWS
GIRDIN MANGBER	SAMJE WASTTER
JETAN GHEIL	YTON TRISCU

KNOCKOUT

In the puzzle below, cross out any word that is described by the clues. When you're done, read top to bottom and left to right to get a quote by George Carlin.

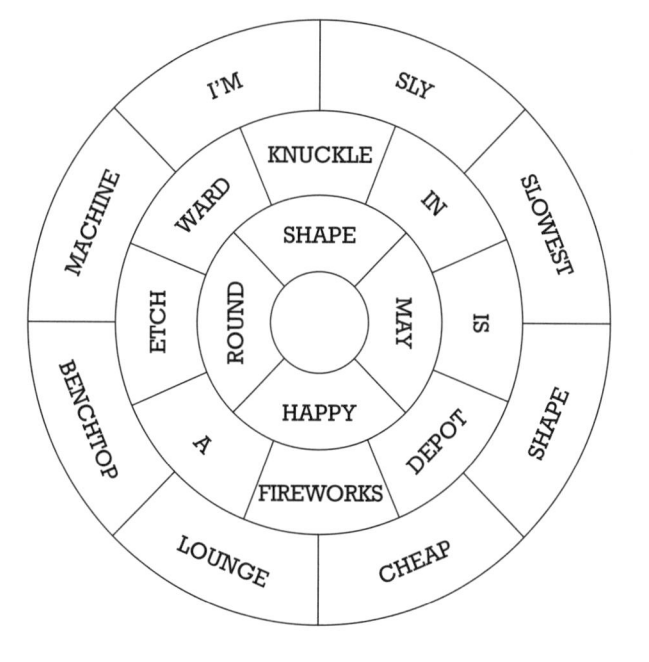

CROSS OUT THE WORD THAT:

1 Is a month of the year.
2 Is "draw" spelled backward.
3 Contains a body part.
4 Is a fruit, with the letters mixed up.
5 Has a silent "K."
6 Changes the meaning of the word if you add "low" after the first letter.
7 Is the name of one of the Seven Dwarfs.
8 Can come after wr- or before -ing.
9 Contains a direction.
10 Has the pattern CVCCCCVC, if C = consonant and V = vowel.
11 Looks like it means "take out of a vessel," but it's a garage.
12 Can mean a burst of temper or a burst of light.
13 Is two different words if you read every other letter.

Anyone who stops learning is old, whether at 20 or 80. Anyone who keeps learning stays young.

—Henry Ford

SAME LETTER
START "P"

Answer as many of these seven-letter words that begin with "P" as you can. For an extra challenge, give yourself a time limit. When you're done, read down the highlighted diagonal for another seven-letter "P" word.

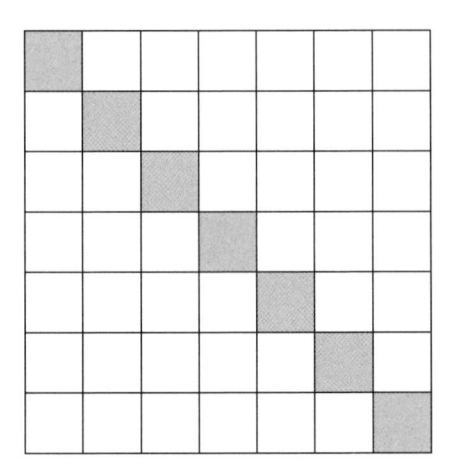

Clue							
Knee bone							
Artist's paint holder							
Sidekick							
Result of a foul							
Winged horse							
Ancient Egyptian king							
Knotty snack							

"P" WORD ....

The brain is like a muscle. When it is in use we feel very good. Understanding is joyous.

— Dr. Carl Sagan

MEDIUM

SCRAMBLE
ANAGRAMS

Unscramble the letters within the words below. Then, rearrange the highlighted letters to form the mystery word that completes the quip.

MRAHE   _ _ _ _ _

TLING   _ _ _ _ _

CEWTI   _ _ _ _ _

TEARI   _ _ _ _ _

CEENI   _ _ _ _ _

A day without sunshine is like, you know, _ _ _ _ _ _.
—*Steve Martin*

AAILMS   _ _ _ _ _ _

EECPIA   _ _ _ _ _ _

YDERSS   _ _ _ _ _ _

EECRON   _ _ _ _ _ _

EESSAM   _ _ _ _ _ _

AGNAED   _ _ _ _ _ _

There's no I in _ _ _ _ _ _ _.
— *Peter Serafinowicz*

SENIOR

MIND
GYM
83

MEDICAL
ETYMOLOGY

So many medical words come from Latin and Greek. The word "anatomy," for example, comes from the Greek for "up" (*ana*) and "cutting" (*tome*). Use the glossary to work out which of the meanings below go with the medical words opposite.

GLOSSARY

derm	skin
ecto	outside
endo	inside
epi	upon/outside
hypo	under/less
hyper	above/more
morph	shape
ology	study of
oxi	oxygen
scope	watch/look
steth	chest
stoma	opening/mouth
tension	pressure
therm	heat
trich	hair
xero	dry

MEANINGS

abnormal hair growth
dry mouth
dry skin
high blood pressure
lean body shape
look at the chest
look inside the body
low temperature
outer skin
overheating
under the skin
study of skin
study of structure
too little oxygen

SMART TIP

Squats and push-ups are excellent exercises for physical health, but it seems that they are good for your brain too! It's thought that resistance exercises like these signal to cells in the brain to make new nerve cells, which support brain health. So, that's an extra reason to include these exercises in your routine.

MEDICAL WORDS

hypertension ....

hypothermia ....

stethoscope ....

hypertrichosis ....

ectomorph ....

hypodermic ....

xeroderma ....

endoscopy ....

morphology ....

hyperthermia ....

epidermis ....

xerostomia ....

dermatology ....

hypoxia ....

HARD

BRITISH-STYLE
QUICK CROSSWORD

ACROSS

1 Celestial body (6)
4 Storm drain cover (5)
7 Day in Spain (3)
8 Type of wine (3)
9 Expert (3)
10 Manner (5)
12 Hermit (5)
13 Relate, as a tale (7)
14 Kind person's quality (5, 2, 4)
20 Sailing event (7)
21 Part of TNT, in short (5)
22 Outmoded (5)
25 Sticky stuff (3)
26 25-Across' mirror image (3)
27 Utmost degree (3)
28 Plus (5)
29 Winter Olympics event (6)

DOWN

1 Conditional release (6)
2 Pasta preference (2, 5)
3 Kind of penguin or butterfly (7)
4 Fuel (3)
5 "_____ questions?" (3)
6 Soccer (football) squad (6)
7 Levelheaded (4, 2, 5)
11 Human trunk (5)
15 Vigilant (5)
16 Military rank (7)
17 To the side (7)
18 Card game or span (6)
19 Type of drum (6)
23 Wee child (3)
24 Stuff of genetics (3)

A clear conscience is the sure sign of a bad memory.

—Mark Twain

UNKNOWABLE
NUMBERS

Can you answer the following questions about cars? As a solving aid, the letter of the answer will spell something appropriate.

1 The Ford Model T is still one of the best-selling cars of all time. How many were sold?
   a 15,000,000   **b** 1,500,000   **c** 150,000   **d** 15,000

2 When was the first fuel-powered car produced?
   t 1760   **u** 1885   **v** 1807   **w** 1910

3 How long is the world's shortest car?
   q 7.6 feet (2.3m)   **r** 6.6 feet (2m)   **s** 5.6 feet (1.7m)   **t** 4.6 feet (1.4m)

4 How fast could the Benz Motorwagen, the first practical car, go at top speed?
   m 31mph (50km/h)   **n** 3mph (5km/h)   **o** 6mph (10km/h)   **p** 16mph (26km/h)

5 What year was the first auto race held?
   l 1900   **m** 1895   **n** 1916   **o** 1908

6 About how fast can the world's fastest diesel car go?
   o 350mph (563km/h)   **p** 450mph (724km/h)   **q** 250mph (402km/h)
   r 550mph (885km/h)

7 What year did the Land Rover debut at the World's Fair in Amsterdam?
   a 1928   **b** 1948   **c** 1938   **d** 1918

8 How many Aston Martins were destroyed during the making of the James Bond movie *Quantum of Solace*?
   i 7   **j** 17   **k** 27   **l** 37

9 As of 2021, the 1962 Ferrari 250 GTO is the most expensive car ever sold at auction. What price did it fetch?
   i US$48,400   **j** US$484,000   **k** US$4,840,000   **l** US$48,400,000

10 The Volkswagen Beetle is one of the most popular cars ever made. How many have been sold?
   c 235,000   **d** 2,350,000   **e** 23,500,000   **f** 235,000,000

PICTURE
FILL IN THE BLANKS

Name the foods in the pictures, then fit them into the letters below to make words. The inserted word will never be the beginning or end of the word, but it's up to you to figure out where the word fits. How many can you complete?

DD	....	
HAIRTH	....	
BED	....	
COMPNT	....	
BOCK	....	
RAGAS	....	

IMMENT	....	
SFUL	....	
APANCE	....	
SD	....	
SNESS	....	
REBING	....	

SPOT THE
HIDDEN OBJECTS

Oh no! Grandma has lost her sewing kit in the kitchen. Can you help her find the objects that she has lost? The contents of her sewing kit are listed at the bottom of the page.

BUTTON
KNITTING NEEDLES
PIN
PIN CUSHION
RULER

SAFETY PIN
SCISSORS
THIMBLE
THREAD
YARN BALL

CIRCULAR
FILL IN THE BLANKS

To solve these puzzles, add a letter to the blank space in each circle to make a seven-letter word. You'll have to figure out whether the word is winding around in a clockwise or counterclockwise direction. And you'll have to decide where the word starts within the circle. To aid in solving, the letters that you fill in will spell a six-letter word.

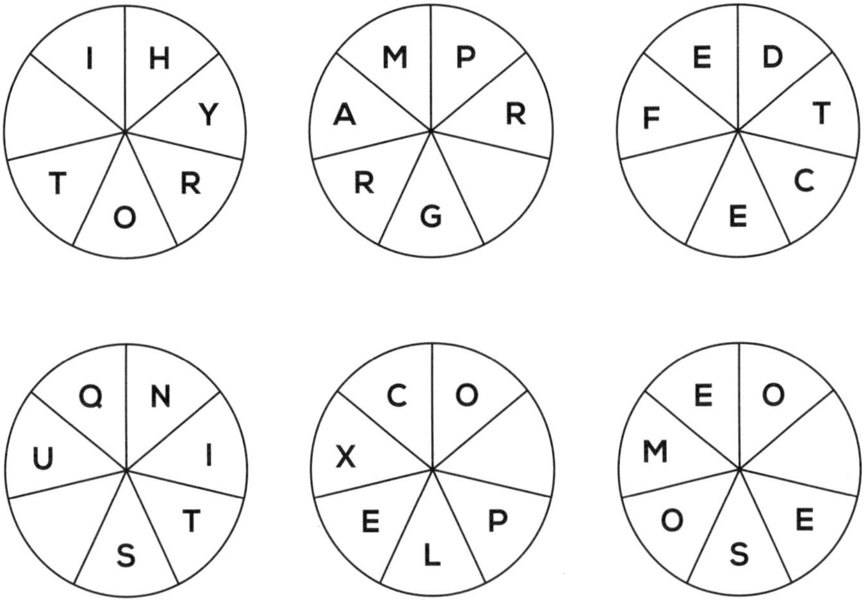

SIX-LETTER WORD ....

OCEANIC
CROSSWORD

ACROSS

1 Bathe
5 Throws in
9 Name of eight English kings
14 Bikini, for one
15 Snare
16 Zinc _____ (sunblock ingredient)
17 Clothes line
18 *Stormy Weather* singer Horne
19 En _____ (as a group)
20 Delighted (US phrase)
23 Part of RSVP
24 Brain scan letters
25 Medical suffix meaning "condition"
28 Make haste
31 French summers
33 Equipped
35 River of Pakistan
37 Han of *Star Wars*
39 Indian flatbread
40 One who doesn't fit in
43 London art gallery
44 Cock-_____ (mixed dog breed)
45 Poet TS
46 Hooded parka
48 Gumbo veggie
50 Blubber
51 Env. contents
52 Something you don't want to get thrown under?
54 Poivre's partner
55 Become ridiculous, as a TV series
61 Clark's colleague
64 Historical periods
65 Burn soother
66 Martini garnish

67 Former Italian currency
68 Doctor's measure
69 _____ up (evaluated)
70 Cuts off
71 Lennon of the Beatles

DOWN

1 Fond hope
2 On the briny, or where you'd find part of 20-, 40- or 55-Across
3 Smack
4 Rope fiber
5 "Finally!" (2 words)
6 Puts on a tux, for example
7 American personalites Carvey or Delany
8 The final frontier
9 Tribute
10 Final
11 _____ *for Noose* (Sue Grafton novel) (2 words)
12 Ave. crossers
13 "_____-haw!"
21 "Holy cow!" (US expression)
22 _____ lamb
25 Steamy
26 Shooting star
27 _____ snowball (comet)
28 _____ hernia
29 Baby
30 Publishing professional
32 "I thought _____"
34 Uzbekistan's _____ Sea
36 _____-friendly
38 After someone has 6-Down, they probably have this effect

41 Caulking made from 4-Down
42 Welts
47 Mistreated
49 _____ pieces
53 Hex
55 Jazz jargon
56 Small musical combo
57 Pilgrimage to Mecca
58 Sag _____ (curried spinach
   and potatoes)

59 _____ Hashanah
60 Avid
61 _____ Angeles
62 Inventor Whitney
63 Guru

ADD -ING
TO A MOVIE TITLE

Adding -ing to a movie title allows us to reimagine the plot of the movie. Can you match the funny plot change to the original movies listed at the bottom of the page? For example, the plot "a six-year-old tells the story of how she dealt with her first year at school" could be matched to KINDERGARTEN COP to make KINDERGARTEN COPING.

1 How can a T. Rex, with its ridiculously short arms, run an auto lot in the city? Find out in this tense thriller.

2 A German man wants to sell his house. Will it be purchased?

3 A sad tale about a guy whose best friend has stopped talking to him. This has all the angst you'd expect in a teenage film.

4 Will he mismatch on this attempt to do up his sweater? Find out in this quirky movie.

5 Rich people have reserved the rainforest. Will they be able to handle all the animals?

6 After years of fighting, a couple finally straightens out their driveway.

7 A harried mother tries to cook the perfect dinner for all her brood's new diets.

8 A girl makes extra money as a tailor.

9 A large guy goes to the Alps for a vacation.

10 A cautionary documentary about how crabby going without food makes people.

THE BIG LEBOWSKI
THE CURIOUS CASE OF BENJAMIN BUTTON
DUDE, WHERE'S MY CAR?
THE FAST AND THE FURIOUS
GONE WITH THE WIND

THE JUNGLE BOOK
JURASSIC PARK
LILO AND STITCH
THE RIGHT STUFF
SCHINDLER'S LIST

SAME LETTER
START "M"

Answer as many of these six-letter words that begin with "M" as you can. For an extra challenge, give yourself a time limit. When you're done, read down the highlighted diagonal for another six-letter "M" word.

Desert illusion

Lass

Purplish-red

Reason

Instant

Brunch cocktail

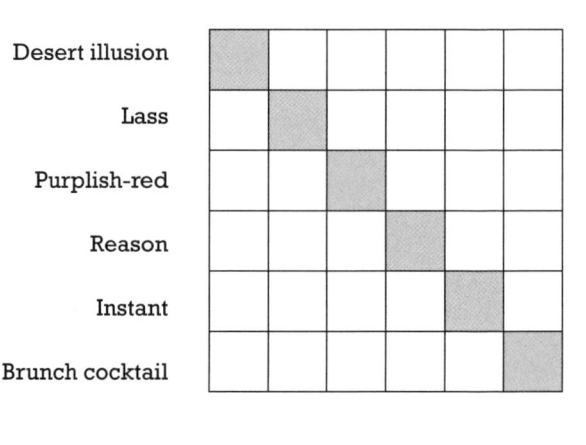

"M" WORD

SMART TIP

Ever noticed that it's easier to memorize lyrics than try to remember the same words on their own? Or, that a smell can conjure up an event or a person you haven't thought about in years? That's because the brain works through associations, so the more senses you involve when you're trying to memorize something, the better.

FAIRY TALES
SCRAMBLE

How much do you know about fairy tales? Find out by reading the questions and finding the answers scrambled at the bottom of the page.

1 This fairy tale has been adapted in many different ways: an animated virtual reality story called *Allumette*, a TV musical, and an animated short film.

2 Gerda and Kai struggle with good and evil in this fable.

3 In this Norweigan tale, the main character foils a witch's attempts to kidnap him.

4 The earliest-known version of this famous story is called *Perceforest* and was written in the 1300s.

5 A common theme in tales is the hero using ingenuity and trickery to overcome a stronger opponent. The animal hero of this tale does this exactly.

6 The main character of this tale lived in a Chinese village and was lazy and greedy at the story's start.

7 This story centers on a rich man who has killed a number of his wives. His newest wife discovers the crimes and has to survive.

8 Another fairy tale features an odd inheritance: a clever animal that helps its master become wealthy. It is an Italian tale dating back to the 1500s.

9 The original German title was *Schneewittchen*.

10 One of Aesop's fables, this tale centers on a god retrieving an axe from a river.

ETH OTORTIES DAN HET RHEA	LGINEEPS YEUABT
HET ONSW EEQUN	OWNS HITEW
HET SHOENT OOTTECURWD	PUTEBCRTU
LAANIDD	TEH TTLEIL CHAMT LIGR
LERBAUBED	UPSS NI OBOST

UNKNOWABLE
NUMBERS: INVENTIONS

Can you answer the following questions about inventions? As a solving aid, the letter of the answer will spell something appropriate.

1 What year was the seismograph invented?
   a 1320   **b** 132   **c** 1832   **d** 1932

2 How many Pet Rocks were sold in 1975?
   r 1,000,000   **s** 10,000   **t** 1,000   **u** 100,000

3 Leonardo da Vinci had the idea for contact lenses in 1508. When were contact lenses successfully produced?
   a 1888   **b** 1918   **c** 1948   **d** 1928

4 How many years ago do we think brain surgery was first performed?
   h 70   **i** 7,000   **j** 700   **k** 70,000

5 What year was the first color film footage recorded?
   n 1899   **o** 1889   **p** 1919   **q** 1929

6 The Tang Dynasty of China is credited with inventing ice cream. Around what year did they add cream to snow from the mountains?
   q 18   **r** 1218   **s** 618   **t** 1618

7 Before Nintendo sold video games, they sold playing cards with Disney characters printed on them. How many did they sell in their first year?
   q 6,000,000   **r** 6,000   **s** 600   **t** 600,000

8 Cornelius van Drebbel built the first working submarine. It was basically a rowboat, but it could go 15 feet (4.6m) below the surface. What year did he build it?
   o 1620   **p** 1820   **q** 1920   **r** 1720

9 The best-selling video game is Minecraft. As of 2021, how many copies have sold?
   o 200,000   **p** 2,000,000   **q** 20,000,000   **r** 200,000,000

10 The first record of paper being used in the bathroom is from China. What year was toilet paper first mentioned?
   k 1589   **l** 1789   **m** 589   **n** 1089

TRIVIA
MATCHING

Starting at the top of the left-hand column and working your way down, match the movie to its leading lady by drawing a line to join the dots next to each one. When you're done, read the letters you've crossed, in the order you crossed them, to find a phrase.

TITANIC •
CASABLANCA •
PSYCHO •
ENCHANTED •
ROCKY •
CHICAGO •
ALIEN •
GHOST •
SPEED •
GREASE •

B D E E R B O R E L G T H M E E N A I C D G D L L I Q Y A Y T W A L D O K F O U T N P E W R A U H E I F A C D S F

• RENEE ZELLWEGER
• SIGOURNEY WEAVER
• SANDRA BULLOCK
• KATE WINSLET
• DEMI MOORE
• INGRID BERGMAN
• JANET LEIGH
• AMY ADAMS
• OLIVIA NEWTON-JOHN
• TALIA SHIRE

ANSWER ....

Egotism, *n*: Doing the *New York Times* crossword puzzle with a pen.

— Ambrose Bierce

SCRAMBLE
ANAGRAMS

Unscramble the letters within the words below. Then, rearrange the highlighted letters to form the mystery word that completes each quip.

LIICET   _ _ _ _ _ _

AAATVR   _ _ _ _ _ _

NNTTEA   _ _ _ _ _ _

EESRTO   _ _ _ _ _ _

CAARBS   _ _ _ _ _ _

ORDAFE   _ _ _ _ _ _

Haircuts are great because I did none of the work but get all of the _ _ _ _ _ _ _.
—*Ludwig Pettersson*

EEEMNTL   _ _ _ _ _ _ _

WWKDRAA   _ _ _ _ _ _ _

AABDNON   _ _ _ _ _ _ _

NITTIAC   _ _ _ _ _ _ _

AMMILDE   _ _ _ _ _ _ _

AEELGSS   _ _ _ _ _ _ _

AANLURT   _ _ _ _ _ _ _

Whoever named it _ _ _ _ _ _ _ _ is a poor judge of anatomy.
—*Groucho Marx*

SENIOR

MIND
GYM

99

EASY

SPOT
THE DIFFERENCE

Can you find ten differences between the images?

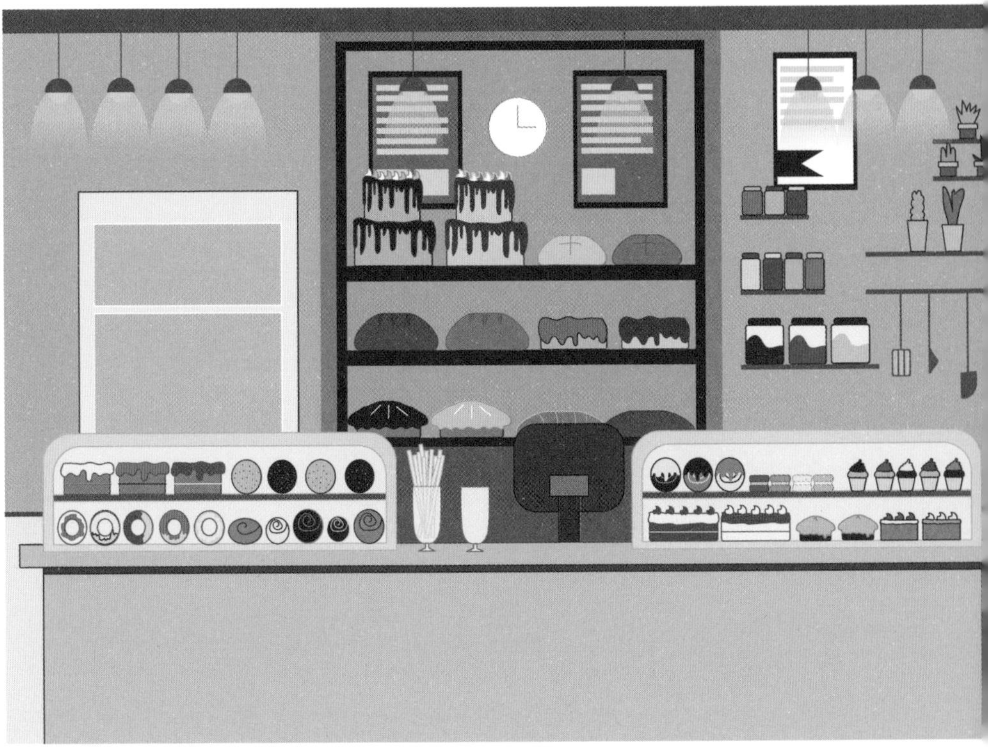

EASY

SPORTS
SCRAMBLE

Can you unscramble the answers to the sports trivia at the bottom of the page?
They are all numbers. Can you match them up? Good luck!

1 How many players are allowed on the ice per team during regular play
in ice hockey?

2 "The turn" in golf takes place after which hole number?

3 How many soccer (football) World Cups has Brazil, the country with the most, won?

4 How many ways are there for a batsman to go out in cricket?

5 How many players compete per team in soccer (football)?

6 In feet, how high is a basketball hoop?

7 How many home runs did baseball great Ty Cobb hit in his three
World Series appearances?

8 How many minutes are you allowed to look for your ball in golf?

9 How many back-to-back strikes does it take to get a turkey in bowling?

10 How many points does a "safety" earn a team in American football?

ENT	THERE
FVEI	WOT
NNIE	VEIF
NTE	VEELNE
ROZE	XSI

CATEGORY
CROSSOUTS

In each grid below, you can take the letters from a square in each column, reading left to right, to make a word. All of the words in a grid belong to the same category. Feel free to cross out the letters, as each square will be used only once. It's up to you to figure out which category goes with which grid.

E	E	T	NE
SA	AR	UR	US
V	P	R	N
NE	A	TU	S
M	T	N	H

LE	OC	I	CE
BR	TT	AT	P
O	R	U	LI
TU	T	CO	ON
PO	N	NI	O

BA	O	IE	ER
C	S	L	T
SP	ST	X	FF
B	OL	SE	L
MA	AN	I	IE

DOGS   PLANETS   VEGETABLES

ONE-LETTER
CHANGE

Look at the pictures below. They represent common three-word sayings with one letter changed.

For example, you could solve this as "Sash is King" and the final answer would be "Cash is King."

Now try these. The altered words are in alphabetical order at the bottom of the page if you need a hint.

....

....

ALTERED WORDS
DAY, GRACE, LIFE, POWER, SHARE

CIRCULAR
FILL IN THE BLANKS

To solve these puzzles, add a letter to the blank space in each circle to make a five-letter word. You'll have to figure out whether the word is winding around in a clockwise or counterclockwise direction. And you'll have to decide where the word starts within the circle. To aid in solving, the letters that you fill in will spell a six-letter word.

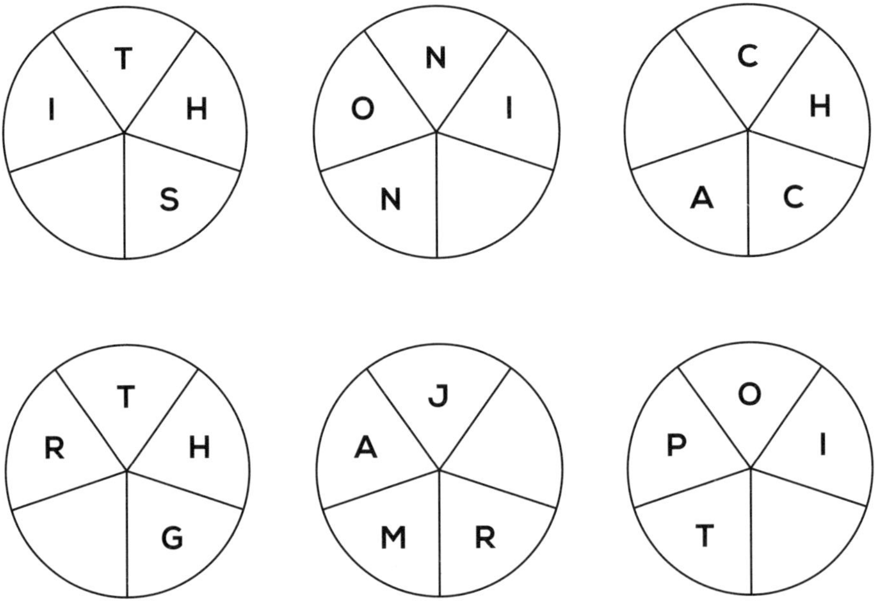

Puzzle 1: T, I, H, S (one blank)

Puzzle 2: N, O, I, N (one blank)

Puzzle 3: C, H, C, A (one blank)

Puzzle 4: T, R, H, G (one blank)

Puzzle 5: J, A, R, M (one blank)

Puzzle 6: O, P, I, T (one blank)

SIX-LETTER WORD ....

ENSEMBLE
CROSSWORD

ACROSS

1 Spicy dip
6 Eye part
10 Require
14 Set _____ of exchange (2 words)
15 Sandwich cookie
16 "Sure!"
17 Pave over again
18 _____ contendere (US court plea)
19 Simple
20 Jewelry-themed 1941 hit by
   55-Across (4 words)
23 Two-speaker system
24 60s psychedelic
25 Like skim milk
29 Eye part
32 (I've Got a Gal in) _____, song by
   55-Across
37 Rocky crag
39 One of the Donald's exes
40 Menagerie
41 Anxious
42 Marisa of My Cousin Vinny
43 1939 hit by 55-Across, chosen by the
   US National Public Radio's list of The
   100 Most Important Music Works of
   the 20th Century (3 words)
45 She sheep
46 Fashionable
48 View
49 Sweetie
55 Orchestra with 16 number-one
   records and 69 top-ten hits, including
   Pennsylvania 6-5000 (3 words)
61 Nothing in tennis
62 Exotic berry used in smoothies

63 Damon and Dillon
64 Mayberry kid or English painter
65 Roll's partner
66 Ablaze
67 Ale
68 Leg joint
69 Bar seat

DOWN

1 Teasdale and Pascoe
2 "Give it _____!" (2 words)
3 Coffee choice
4 Ringo of the Beatles
5 Eagle's home (US spelling)
6 Tedious
7 Buck or kang suffix
8 "To thine own _____ be true"
9 Hubbub
10 Wanderer
11 One who barely squeaks by
12 Nobleman
13 Stains
21 Tetra + five
22 Landed property
26 Actor-musician Nelson
27 Middays
28 Pays, as the bill
29 Jay, once of The Tonight Show
30 "Don't take _____ hard!" (2 words)
31 Exploit
32 Toy with a tail
33 Swear
34 Kind of duck or excuse
35 Chemical suffix
36 Damsel
38 Sleep stage

44 Jekyll's alter ego
47 Comment
48 Scoff
50 Bombeck and Calderon
51 Toward the stern
52 Mathematical proportion
53 Brief opening statement?
54 Famous Ford flop
55 Lump
56 Horse's gait

57 Woman's name that sounds like two letters
58 Trash can on a desktop
59 Tie up
60 Similar

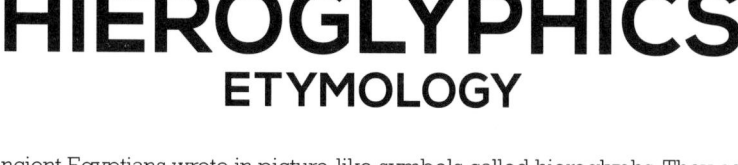

HIEROGLYPHICS
ETYMOLOGY

The ancient Egyptians wrote in picture-like symbols called hieroglyphs. They can represent both images and phonetic sounds. For example, the snake hieroglyph can be the letter "J" or the word "cobra." Using the hieroglyphics glossary, can you work out the message below? Remember, the hieroglyphics can mean a single letter, a sound, or a whole word!

GLOSSARY

A	**A**	**B**	**D**	**E**	**F**	**G**	**H**	**H**	**I**
vulture	arm	leg	hand	reed	snake	jar	wick	reed shelter	-

J	**K**	**M**	**N**	**O**	**P**	**Q**	**R**	**S**	**S**
cobra	basket	owl	water ripple	-	stool	hill	mouth	folded cloth	lock (or) bolt

T	**U**	**U**	**TCH**	**KH**	**SH**	**H**	**N**	**M**	**V**
bread	chick	rope	cord	sieve	pool	belly	crown	rib	-

....

....

....

SPOT THE
HIDDEN OBJECTS

Uh oh! Grandpa has loaned out his tools to all the people in the village. Now he needs them for a project. Can you help him find all the hidden tools? They are listed at the bottom of the page.

CHISEL   SCREWDRIVER
PLIERS   LEVEL
FILE   TROWEL
SAW   PAINTBRUSH
HAMMER   WRENCH

HARD

CATEGORY
CROSSOUTS

In each grid, you can take the letters from a square in each column, reading left to right, to make a word. All of the words in a grid belong to the same category. Feel free to cross out the letters, as each square will be used only once. It's up to you to figure out which category goes with which grid.

SP	A	V	K
L	CE	IN	ER
O	R	K	N
C	I	E	M
S	RE	EA	E
R	TR	A	G

M	A	TE	N
K	I	D	R
S	AS	OO	ER
L	N	X	E
S	P	TU	LE
TO	PA	IF	LA

T	A	RR	ER
TR	CY	I	N
F	A	UC	I
BI	R	X	Y
T	OO	CL	K
SC	E	T	E

KITCHEN
TRANSPORT
WATER

ANCIENT
HISTORY QUIZ

1 A Roman Emperor was once captured by pirates and held for ransom. He insisted that the ransom was too small. He also vowed to hunt them down and kill them all after it was paid. True to his word, he did find them and crucify them. Who was he?
a Julius Caesar   **b** Nero   **c** Claudius Caesar   **d** Augustus Caesar

2 What did the Romans build to defend the northern border of their empire?
a The Colossus of Rhodes   **b** London Bridge   **c** Hadrian's Wall
d The Colosseum

3 People from Asia, Anatolia, and Africa mixed with Minoan settlers on an island in the Mediterranean. It is believed that this island is where the Greek civilization originated. Which island is it?
a Sardinia   **b** Cyprus   **c** Malta   **d** Crete

4 In the 6th century BCE, a philosopher is credited with making the first map of the world. Who was he?
a Anaximander   **b** Socrates   **c** Archimedes   **d** Plato

5 Yu the Great founded the Xia Dynasty of China. It lasted for hundreds of years, with 17 kings and 14 generations of rulers. What was Yu's claim to fame?
a He had 90 children   **b** He built flood controls   **c** He built the Great Wall
d He was 7 feet (2m) tall

6 Which age came after the Stone Age?
a Bronze Age   **b** Iron Age   **c** Paleolithic Age   **d** Neolithic Age

7 Which structure was built during the Old Kingdom in Egypt?
a Tower of Babel   **b** Sphinx   **c** Hanging Gardens of Babylon   **d** Statue of Zeus

8 Which culture has the oldest verified alphabet?
a Romans   **b** Greek   **c** Vikings   **d** Phoenicians

9 Which city was the first to reach a population of one million?
a Mexico City   **b** Cairo   **c** Rome   **d** London

10 Which of the following did the ancient Egyptians NOT invent?
a Clocks   **b** Toothpaste   **c** Ox-drawn plow   **d** Kites

NAME
THE OBJECTS

Here are some oddly named objects. See how many you can name. When you're done, reading down the first letters will name another odd object.

....

....

....

....

....

....

OBJECT

....

TURNABOUT

Place the answer to the clue in the appropriately numbered row. Enter the answer until you run out of room, then keep going in the following row, going backward. This backward piece will be the beginning of the next answer.

Example: The first word is POTS. The last two letters wrap around into the second row. The second word is STEP. The third word is PEER. And the fourth word is REPO, wrapping back up to the top.

P	O
S	T
P	E
R	E

1 Group spirit

2 Thrilled

3 Loathe

4 African fly menace

5 Look up to

6 More timid

7 Repair, as mittens

8 Glittery Christmas decoration

9 Landlord

10 Team list

11 Laces again

12 Fishing nets

13 Felt

14 Sahara, e.g.

15 Quake

1		
2		
3		
4		
5		
6		
7		
8		
9		
10		
11		
12		
13		
14		
15		

ESCAPE
THE BOOK

Time to escape the book! First, you're going to gather all the exit codes from the Escape the Page puzzles. Write the numbers of the exit codes in the top of each box. Do that here:

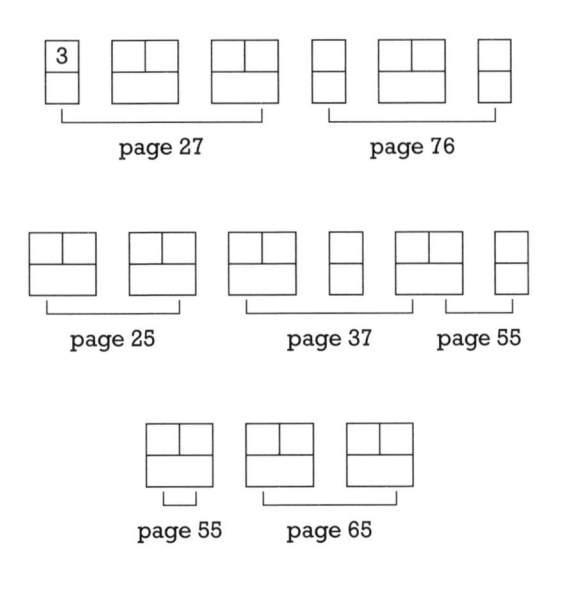

page 27   page 76

page 25   page 37   page 55

page 55   page 65

Now, using the grid below, convert the numbers to letters to find the first part of the hidden message.

1	2	3	4	5	6	7	8	9	10	11	12	13	14	15	16	17	18	19	20	21	22	23	24	25	26
A	B	C	D	E	F	G	H	I	J	K	L	M	N	O	P	Q	R	S	T	U	V	W	X	Y	Z

You'll find these samples from puzzles somewhere in this book. Once you've located them, write the circled letter under each sample to reveal the second part of the hidden message.

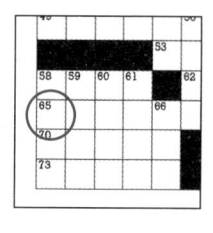

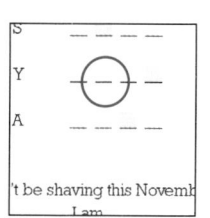

....

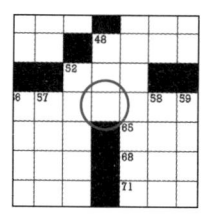

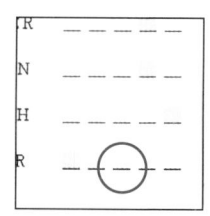

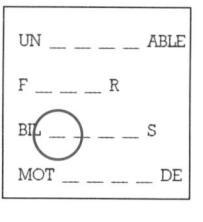

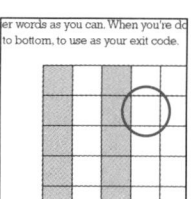

....

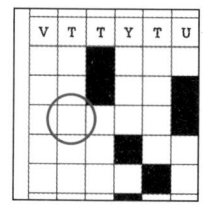

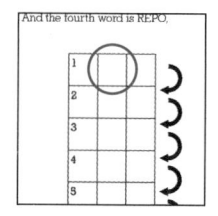

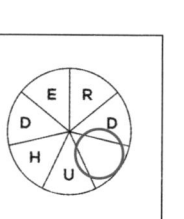

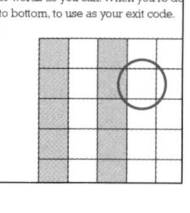

....

ANSWERS

PAGE 8

YOKO ONO—JOHN LENNON / CLEOPATRA—MARC ANTONY / BONNIE—CLYDE / MISS PIGGY—KERMIT / MARGE—HOMER / OLIVE OYL—POPEYE / MINNIE—MICKEY / LAUREN BACALL—HUMPHREY BOGART / KATHERINE HEPBURN—SPENCER TRACY / PRINCESS LEIA—HAN SOLO / **"YOU COMPLETE ME"**

PAGE 9

C	A	T
O	R	E
W	E	D

D	O	G
A	N	O
B	E	D

A	N	T
B	O	O
E	W	E

PAGE 10

```
F L A G ▓ P E T A L ▓ P I N K
L U G E ▓ A M A N I ▓ E M I N
A X E R ▓ ▓ T E N A M ▓ P O N E
P E R I W I N K L E ▓ S A N E
▓ ▓ R O D S ▓ ▓ V I N Y L
D A I S Y ▓ ▓ I N I ▓ ▓
A L S O ▓ A I S L E D ▓ O D E
L I L Y O F T H E V A L L E Y
L T E ▓ P A L A T E ▓ I D L E
▓ U R L ▓ ▓ M E S A S
L O T U S ▓ ▓ D O O M ▓
A N O N ▓ S N A P D R A G O N
S E M I ▓ N O M A D ▓ N E M O
E T A T ▓ A T O L L ▓ T A N G
R O S E ▓ P A N S Y ▓ I R I S
```

PAGE 12

Crossword answers include: DON JOHN / TITANIA / PUCK / MERCUTIO / ROSALIND / TITUS ANDRONICUS / KING LEAR / JULIUS CAESAR / JULIET CAPULET / OPHELIA / ROMEO MONTAGUE / MARC ANTONY

PAGE 13

WHITEN / VORTEX / HOCKEY / FUNNEL / ACTION / SHADOW / **TRENCH**

PAGE 14

WHERE MONSTERS ROAM

PAGE 15
1. BRUNO / 2. EVA / 3. CASSIDY /
4. DEAN / 5. GINA / 6. HENRY /
7. FREDDY / 8. ANGELINA

PAGE 16
1. b / 2. a / 3. d / 4. TRUE / 5. TRUE /
6. FALSE / 7. TRUE / 8. d / 9. c / 10. a

PAGE 17
CARRIAGE / ODOMETER /
MAGNIFYING GLASS / PRETZELS /
ABACUS / STETHOSCOPE / SHAMROCK
/ **COMPASS**

PAGE 18
MICROPHONE / ENLARGE A PHOTO /
TAKE A PHOTO / EMAIL / ANGEL
/ PROJECTOR / PLAYGROUND /
CARDBOARD BOX / RADIO / TOY BOX /
BRAINSTORM / FUSE BOX / COMPUTER
/ LIGHTNING

PAGE 20

P	G	A		S	T	E	L	A		R	O	Y	A	L
O	E	R		E	A	T	E	N		E	N	E	R	O
E	N	E		E	X	U	D	E		L	I	N	G	O
M	E	N		K	I	N	G	S	R	A	N	S	O	M
S	T	A	G			E	T	A	T					
		A	I	R			S	E	E	S	A	W		
A	N	A	S	T	A	S	I	A		N	I	T	E	
J	A	C	K	O	F	A	L	L	T	R	A	D	E	S
A	M	I	E		P	L	A	C	E	M	E	N	T	
R	E	D	T	A	G		M	M	E					
		N	D	A	K			L	A	C	E			
Q	U	E	E	N	S	B	E	R	R	Y		G	A	M
U	L	T	R	A		A	B	E	A	M		E	N	O
I	N	A	L	L		T	O	N	I	C		N	O	T
P	A	L	E	S		E	B	O	L	A		T	E	E

PAGE 22
1. a / 2. c / 3. d / 4. c / 5. b / 6. b / 7. a /
8. c / 9. d / 10. b

PAGE 24
MARINE / MORALE / MASCOT /
MENACE / MEMOIR / MANIAC /
MOSAIC

PAGE 25
2021

PAGE 26
WHEN I DIE, I WANT TO DIE
LIKE MY GRANDFATHER WHO
DIED PEACEFULLY IN HIS SLEEP,
NOT SCREAMING LIKE ALL THE
PASSENGERS IN HIS CAR.
—WILL ROGERS

PAGE 27
31514

PAGE 28
1. BLUE URANIUM / 2. GREEN
QUARTZ / 3. DANDELION TOPAZ /
4. AQUA VIRIDINE / 5. FUCHSIA RUBY /
6. CREAM PEARL / 7. ECRU SAPPHIRE /
8. HONEY OPAL

PAGE 29
YOU CAN'T HAVE EVERYTHING.
WHERE WOULD YOU PUT IT?
—STEVEN WRIGHT

PAGE 30

O	B	E	L	I	S	K	■	S	E	N	S	E
C	■	L	■	C	■	A	■	P	■	I	■	L
E	M	O	T	I	O	N	■	I	M	A	G	E
A	■	P	■	L	■	G	I	N	■	G	■	M
N	E	E	D	Y	■	A	■	A	W	A	K	E
■	T	■	I	■	R	■	C	■	R	■	N	
C	H	A	N	G	E	O	F	H	E	A	R	T
A	■	R	■	A	■	O	■	L	■	O		
B	E	T	E	L	■	C	■	F	L	A	I	R
A	■	I	■	L	E	O	■	R	■	L	■	O
R	A	S	T	A	■	U	N	I	F	O	R	M
E	■	A	■	N	■	R	■	A	■	H	■	E
T	E	N	E	T	■	T	O	R	N	A	D	O

PAGE 32

FUNNY MONEY—COMEDIAN'S PAY / FURRY PURRY—CAT / HEARTY STARTY—DEFIBRILLATOR / HEATIE FEETIES—SOCKS / LICKIE STICKIE—STAMP / MAYBE BABY—PREGNANCY TEST / PEEPER KEEPER—GLASSES CASE / QUICKIE STICKIE—SUPERGLUE / SCOOPY SOUPY—SPOON / SCREAMY DREAMY—NIGHTMARE / STABBY GRABBY—FORK / WORDIE BIRDIE—PARROT

PAGE 33

GOLD / CYAN / OPAL / JADE / ROAN / TEAL / SAGE / RUST / RUBY

PAGE 34

DRAFT, SALAD, BLAND, RATIO, ALBUM, **DRAMA** / LASSO, ARENA, TENET, TEETH, PRESS, **PHONE**

PAGE 35

1. PINK LOZENGE (3RD ROW, CENTER) / 2. ORANGE AND BLUE FISH (4TH ROW, FAR RIGHT)

PAGE 36

ALWAYS FORGIVE YOUR ENEMIES, NOTHING ANNOYS THEM SO MUCH. —OSCAR WILDE
ALL MEN ARE EQUAL BEFORE FISH. —HERBERT HOOVER

PAGE 37

1212

PAGE 38

I INTEND TO LIVE FOREVER. SO FAR SO GOOD. —STEVEN WRIGHT

PAGE 39

1. WHEN YOU WISH UPON A STAR / 2. (I'VE HAD) THE TIME OF MY LIFE / 3. CAN YOU FEEL THE LOVE TONIGHT? / 4. MRS. ROBINSON / 5. MY HEART WILL GO ON / 6. MOON RIVER / 7. STAYIN' ALIVE / 8. OVER THE RAINBOW / 9. CHEEK TO CHEEK / 10. AS TIME GOES BY

PAGE 40

1. g / 2. a / 3. s / 4. t / 5. r / 6. o / 7. n / 8. o 9. m / 10. y / **GASTRONOMY**

PAGE 41

PASSWORD / JET SKI / LAPTOP / CROSSWORD / PARTY / AMERICA / PEANUTS / KETCHUP / PATCHWORK / WHISKEY / COMPUTER / PANTSUIT / VODKA / TEXT

PAGE 42

1. D / 2. E / 3. C / 4. I / 5. M / 6. A / 7. L / 8. R U N

PAGE 43

SOME PEOPLE SEE THE GLASS HALF FULL. OTHERS SEE IT HALF EMPTY. I SEE A GLASS THAT'S TWICE AS BIG AS IT NEEDS TO BE.
—GEORGE CARLIN

PAGE 44

1	3	2	4	7	9	5	8	6
5	9	8	1	6	2	4	3	7
7	6	4	5	3	8	9	1	2
4	2	7	9	1	3	8	6	5
9	1	5	6	8	7	2	4	3
6	8	3	2	5	4	7	9	1
8	7	1	3	4	5	6	2	9
3	4	9	7	2	6	1	5	8
2	5	6	8	9	1	3	7	4

PAGE 45

CREDIT / SCREEN / GOLDEN / DOLLAR / DANGER / TAVERN / **CELLAR**

PAGE 46

1. a / 2. d / 3. b / 4. d / 5. d / 6. a / 7. c / 8. a / 9. c / 10. d

PAGE 47

IF YOU LIVE TO BE ONE HUNDRED, YOU'VE GOT IT MADE. VERY FEW PEOPLE DIE PAST THAT AGE.
—GEORGE BURNS

PAGE 48

PAGE 49

CZAR, ALAS, OBEY, OPAL, **LAZY** / BEET, BLOB, TALL, ECHO, **BELT**

PAGE 50

ERITREA—ASMARA / CHINA—
BEIJING / JORDAN—AMMAN / EAST
TIMOR—DILI / GUAM—HAGATNA /
ESTONIA—TALLINN / LIBYA—TRIPOLI /
MALTA—VALLETTA / NEW ZEALAND—
WELLINGTON / FIJI—SUVA /
**"THERE ARE NO CAPITALS THAT
START WITH 'X'"**

PAGE 52

P	Y	R	A	M	I	D		A	G	E	N	T
I		E		A		R	U	T		L		A
R	E	M	O	R	S	E		O	P	I	U	M
A		O		Z		S		M		T		E
T	E	D		I	L	S	A		Y	E	A	R
E		E		P		E		P			C	
S	A	L	T	A	N	D	P	E	P	P	E	R
	S			N		T		T		I		O
S	H	O	E		N	O	S	E		N	I	L
E		B		S		K		R		K		L
D	R	E	A	M		I	M	P	R	E	S	S
A		S		E	E	L		A		Y		I
N	I	E	C	E		L	A	N	T	E	R	N

PAGE 54

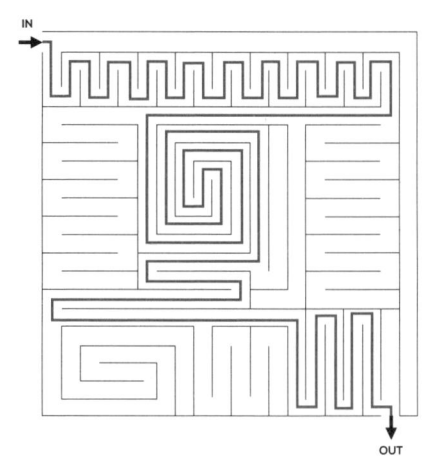

PAGE 55

0915

PAGE 56

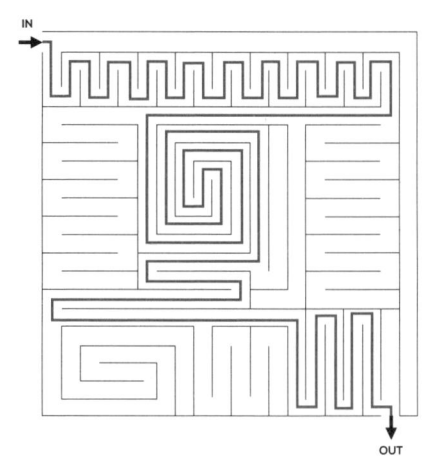

PAGE 57

1. TROY STORY / 2. DIET HARD /
3. I'M RON, MAN / 4. SNAKES ON
A PLANET / 5. PANT MAN / 6. THE
GREEN SMILE / 7. THE MAIZE RUNNER /
8. STAIR WARS / 9. FRIGHT CLUB /
10. SINGIN' IN THE DRAIN

PAGE 58

PIONEER / SELTZER / MERMAID /
SLEIGHT / AWESOME / ARSENAL
/ **PRAISE**

PAGE 59

SET, ION, TOE, **ONE**

PAGE 60
TREES—ASPEN / MAPLE / SPRUCE / WALNUT / **FISH**—ANCHOVY / MARLIN / PERCH / SALMON / TROUT / **FLOWERS**—AZALEA / BEGONIA / CROCUS / ORCHID / TULIP

PAGE 62
The long answers each have one of the primary colors in them.

```
A L A R M ■ A M O S ■ A P E S
D O R I A ■ L I P O ■ H A V E
A S I C S ■ E D E N ■ A T E E
R E D H E R R I N G S ■ E N D
■ ■ ■ R A T ■ P E S T S
S P I N A L ■ O C E A N ■
M O N E T ■ T R A M ■ A L L A
O N C E I N A B L U E M O O N
G E L D ■ A X I L ■ M E D I A
■ L A Y I T ■ S I L E N T
A S H E N ■ ■ B O S ■
B H O ■ Y E L L O W S T O N E
L A N E ■ C I E L ■ A R B O R
E R E S ■ H E E D ■ R E I N A
R E Y S ■ O U R S ■ Y E T I S
```

PAGE 64
PERU / LAOS / MALI / CUBA / OMAN / IRAN / CHAD / LIBYA / NIGER / CHILE / CHINA / SPAIN / MALTA / NEPAL / QATAR / BENIN / TONGA / POLAND / ANGOLA / FRANCE

PAGE 65
EARTH / JUPITER / MERCURY / MARS / NEPTUNE / PLUTO / SATURN / SOLAR SYSTEM / URANUS / VENUS
(Hidden message in the uncircled letters)
FOURTEEN NINETEEN IS YOUR ORBITAL EXIT CODE

PAGE 66
SEDAN / SMILE / STAGE / SNORE / SWEET / **SMART**

PAGE 67
RESTRAINED / BALLERINA / DOLLOP / SCARLET / AUTOPSY / BLOCKADE / LUMBERJACKS / TOUSLED

PAGE 68
PINE / ROWAN / ELM / ASPEN / BEECH / GUM / FIR / TEAK / PALM / ALDER

PAGE 69
RED, YES, CUE, TRY, **USER** / OUT, TOT, NOR, AXE, **TONE**

PAGE 70
1. LEFT TO RIGHT: BOWSER, ALFIE, DINO, CARLY / 2. LEFT TO RIGHT AND TOP TO BOTTOM: JOSS, MOOSE, FRASIER, HOPS, GRETA, INIGO, EDDIE, NETTA, KRAKEN

PAGE 71
ZOO—ELEPHANT / GORILLA / LION / PANDA / RHINO / **BREAKFAST**—BACON / MUFFIN / PANCAKE / SAUSAGE / WAFFLE / **FRUIT**—APPLE / BANANA / GRAPE / LEMON / PEACH

PAGE 72

1. SUDOKU / 2. REPAID / 3. MATCH / 4. TIDYING / 5. SUBTLE / 6. PAT / 7. ROOK / 8. FORM / 9. STATIC / 10. STRETCH / "MY FAVORITE MACHINE AT THE GYM IS THE VENDING MACHINE." —CAROLINE RHEA

PAGE 73

1. DEER / 2. REDO / 3. ODOR / 4. ROAR / 5. RAIL / 6. LION / 7. NODE

PAGE 74

R	A	H		R	A	S	T	A		G	O	M	B	E
E	L	Y		A	S	C	A	M		E	R	I	E	S
L	T	E		C	H	I	M	P	A	N	Z	E	E	S
Y	A	N	N	I			E	L	L		O	N	T	O
	R	A	I	N	F	O	R	E	S	T				
	G	E	A	R			O	U	S	T	E	R		
T	I	L	E		A	C	C	T		N	A	I	V	E
I	S	A	R	T		A	P	E		A	F	L	I	P
E	L	S	I	E		S	A	S	H		A	L	L	S
R	E	H	A	S	H			L	E	E	R			
		T	A	N	G	A	N	Y	I	K	A			
A	L	A	S		L	O	A			E	S	A	L	E
J	A	N	E	G	O	O	D	A	L	L		N	I	P
A	T	O	N	E		N	O	S	E	E		Y	A	P
R	E	N	D	S		E	T	E	X	T		E	S	S

PAGE 76

STEAM / EXILE / VEGAN / ETHIC / NOTCH / OZONE / NANNY / EVENT—7181

PAGE 77

HOWLING / STANDOFFISH / UNBEARABLE / WRATH / FEMUR / VAMOOSE / BILLIONS / DISROBING / MOTORCADE / INFANTRY / LOCATE / EPIGLOTTIS

PAGE 78

SCUFFLE / HUNDRED / FACEOFF / BLANKET / POLYGON / REBUILD— **ENABLE**

PAGE 79

1. DEBBIE REYNOLDS / 2. KATHARINE HEPBURN / 3. TONY CURTIS / 4. JAMES STEWART / 5. INGRID BERGMAN / 6. JAMES DEAN / 7. JANET LEIGH / 8. YUL BRYNNER / 9. ORSON WELLES / 10. ANNE BAXTER

PAGE 80

1. MAY / 2. WARD / 3. MACHINE (CHIN) / 4. CHEAP (PEACH) / 5. KNUCKLE / 6. SLY (SLOWLY) / 7. HAPPY / 8. ETCH / 9. SLOWEST / 10. BENCHTOP / 11. DEPOT / 12. FIREWORKS / 13. LOUNGE / "I'M IN SHAPE. ROUND IS A SHAPE."

PAGE 82

PATELLA / PALETTE / PARTNER / PENALTY / PEGASUS / PHARAOH / PRETZEL / **PARASOL**

PAGE 83

HAREM, GLINT, TWICE, IRATE, NIECE —**NIGHT** / SALAMI, APIECE, DRESSY, ENCORE, SESAME, AGENDA—**DENIAL**

PAGE 84

HIGH BLOOD PRESSURE / LOW TEMPERATURE / LOOK AT THE CHEST / ABNORMAL HAIR GROWTH / LEAN BODY SHAPE / UNDER THE SKIN / DRY SKIN / LOOK INSIDE THE BODY / STUDY OF STRUCTURE / OVERHEATING / OUTER SKIN / DRY MOUTH / STUDY OF SKIN / TOO LITTLE OXYGEN

PAGE 86

P	L	A	N	E	T			G	R	A	T	E
A		L		M		D	I	A		N		L
R	E	D		P	R	O		S	T	Y	L	E
O		E		E		W		O		O		V
L	O	N	E	R		N	A	R	R	A	T	E
E		T		O		T		S				N
	H	E	A	R	T	O	F	G	O	L	D	
B		W			E		E		A		T	
R	E	G	A	T	T	A		N	I	T	R	O
I		R			R		E		E		M	
D	A	T	E	D		T	A	R		R	A	T
G		O		N	T	H		A		A		O
E	X	T	R	A			S	L	A	L	O	M

PAGE 88

1. a / 2. u / 3. t / 4. o / 5. m / 6. o / 7. b / 8. i / 9. l / 10. e / **AUTOMOBILE**

PAGE 89

DAPPLED / IMPEACHMENT / HAIRBREADTH / SCORNFUL / BEGGED / APPEARANCE / COMPLIMENT / SPIED / BOOKRACK / SLEEKNESS / RAGAMUFFINS / REPLUMBING

PAGE 90

PAGE 91

HISTORY / PROGRAM / DEFLECT / INQUEST / COMPLEX / SOMEONE / **SOLEMN**

PAGE 92

W	A	S	H		A	D	D	S		H	E	N	R	Y
I	S	L	E		T	R	A	P		O	X	I	D	E
S	E	A	M		L	E	N	A		M	A	S	S	E
H	A	P	P	Y	A	S	A	C	L	A	M			
			E	S	S		E	E	G		E	M	A	
H	I	E		E	T	E	S		G	E	A	R	E	D
I	N	D	U	S		S	O	L	O		R	O	T	I
A	F	I	S	H	O	U	T	O	F	W	A	T	E	R
T	A	T	E		A	P	O	O		E	L	I	O	T
A	N	O	R	A	K		O	K	R	A		C	R	Y
L	T	R		B	U	S		S	E	L				
			J	U	M	P	T	H	E	S	H	A	R	K
L	E	W	I	S		E	R	A	S		A	L	O	E
O	L	I	V	E		L	I	R	E		D	O	S	E
S	I	Z	E	D		L	O	P	S		J	O	H	N

PAGE 94

1. JURASSIC PARKING / 2. SCHINDLER'S LISTING / 3. DUDE, WHERE'S MY CARING? / 4. THE CURIOUS CASE OF BENJAMIN BUTTONING / 5. THE JUNGLE BOOKING / 6. GONE WITH THE WINDING / 7. THE RIGHT STUFFING / 8. LILO AND STITCHING / 9. THE BIG LEBOWSKIING / 10. THE FASTING AND THE FURIOUS

PAGE 95

MIRAGE / MAIDEN / MAROON / MOTIVE / MOMENT / MIMOSA / **MARINA**

PAGE 96

1. THE LITTLE MATCH GIRL / 2. THE SNOW QUEEN / 3. BUTTERCUP / 4. SLEEPING BEAUTY / 5. THE TORTOISE AND THE HARE / 6. ALADDIN / 7. BLUEBEARD / 8. PUSS IN BOOTS / 9. SNOW WHITE / 10. THE HONEST WOODCUTTER

PAGE 97

1. b / 2. r / 3. a / 4. i / 5. n / 6. s / 7. t / 8. o / 9. r / 10. m / **BRAINSTORM**

PAGE 98

TITANIC—KATE WINSLET / CASABLANCA—INGRID BERGMAN / PSYCHO—JANET LEIGH / ENCHANTED—AMY ADAMS / ROCKY —TALIA SHIRE / CHICAGO—RENEE ZELLWEGER / ALIEN—SIGOURNEY WEAVER / GHOST—DEMI MOORE / SPEED—SANDRA BULLOCK / GREASE —OLIVIA NEWTON-JOHN / "**BE THE LEADING LADY OF YOUR OWN LIFE**"

PAGE 99

ELICIT, AVATAR, TENANT, STEREO, SCARAB, FEDORA, **CREDIT** / ELEMENT, AWKWARD, ABANDON, TITANIC, DILEMMA, AGELESS, NATURAL, **NECKING**

PAGE 100

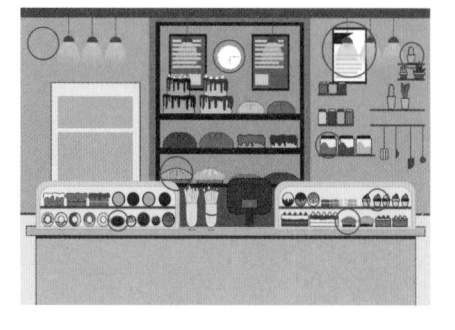

PAGE 102

1. SIX / 2. NINE / 3. FIVE / 4. TEN / 5. ELEVEN / 6. TEN / 7. ZERO / 8. FIVE / 9. THREE / 10. TWO

PAGE 103

PLANETS—EARTH / MARS / NEPTUNE / SATURN / VENUS / **VEGETABLES**— BROCCOLI / LETTUCE / ONION / POTATO / TURNIP / **DOGS**—BASSET / BOXER / COLLIE / MASTIFF / SPANIEL

PAGE 104

SEIZE THE HAY—SEIZE THE DAY / WIFE IS BEAUTIFUL—LIFE IS BEAUTIFUL / KNOWLEDGE IS MOWER— KNOWLEDGE IS POWER / SNARE THE WEALTH—SHARE THE WEALTH / TRACE UNDER PRESSURE—GRACE UNDER PRESSURE

PAGE 105
SMITH / ONION / CATCH / RIGHT /
MAJOR / POINT—**MOTION**

PAGE 106

S	A	L	S	A		L	A	S	H		N	E	E	D
A	R	A	T	E		O	R	E	O		O	K	A	Y
R	E	T	A	R		N	O	L	O		M	E	R	E
A	S	T	R	I	N	G	O	F	P	E	A	R	L	S
S	T	E	R	E	O			L	S	D				
				N	O	N	F	A	T		L	I	D	
K	A	L	A	M	A	Z	O	O		A	R	E	T	E
I	V	A	N	A		Z	O	O		T	E	N	S	E
T	O	M	E	I		I	N	T	H	E	M	O	O	D
E	W	E		D	R	E	S	S	Y					
		S	E	E				D	E	A	R	I	E	
G	L	E	N	N	M	I	L	L	E	R	B	A	N	D
L	O	V	E		A	C	A	I		M	A	T	T	S
O	P	I	E		R	O	C	K		A	F	I	R	E
B	E	E	R		K	N	E	E		S	T	O	O	L

PAGE 108
GIV ME A Hand Wick DIS basket Fowl
OV bread AND chickN / **GIVE ME A
HAND WITH THIS BASKET FULL OF
BREAD AND CHICKEN**

PAGE 109

PAGE 110
WATER—CREEK / LAKE / OCEAN /
RIVER / SPRING / STREAM / **KITCHEN**—
KNIFE / LADLE / MIXER / SPATULA /
SPOON / TOASTER / **TRANSPORT**—
BICYCLE / FERRY / SCOOTER / TAXI /
TRAIN / TRUCK

PAGE 111
1. a / 2. c / 3. b / 4. a / 5. b / 6. a / 7. b /
8. d / 9. c / 10. d

PAGE 112
VIOLET (OR VIOLA) / OCELOT / LARIAT
/ CASINO / ANTLERS / NACHOS /
OTTER / **VOLCANO**

PAGE 113
1. MORALE / 2. ELATED / 3. DETEST /
4. TSETSE / 5. ESTEEM / 6. MEEKER /
7. REKNIT / 8. TINSEL / 9. LESSOR /
10. ROSTER / 11. RETIES / 12. SEINES /
13. SENSED / 14. DESERT / 15. TREMOR

PAGE 114
3 15 14 7 18 1 20 21 12 1 20 9 15 14 19
CONGRATULATIONS

J (p74); O (p30); B (p49); W (p63);
E (p34); L (p77), L (p76); D (p47);
O (p113); N (p78); E (p24)
JOB WELL DONE

ACKNOWLEDGMENTS

I owe everything to my mom, Susan, and my dad, Don. You kindled my love of puzzles at an early age by challenging me with word games, board games, and *Games Magazine*. And you kept me from being a completely bookish person by sending me out to play in the yard. Those hours outside helped foster a creativity and a love of play that has been profoundly important in my professional and personal life.

I'm eternally grateful to my husband, John. I continue to thank my lucky stars that we found each other. The life we've built is full of wonder and discovery, and I can't wait to talk to you every day.

My wonderful boys, Henry and Lewis, inspire me every day. Thanks for being my puzzle guinea pigs from age two to this day. You're going to have great lives and I can't wait to see what you become! Look for all three of my family member's names in the Oceanic Crossword, pages 92–93. I think about you all the time.

Kelly and Dave, you were my first and best playmates, thanks for putting up with me all these years! You've both taught me so much. I'm thankful to have you in my life.

Jennie, a friend like you is more valuable than diamonds. I'm truly blessed to have you in my life. The deep time that we've spent together has been full of adventure and growth. You are my chosen sister and I look forward to our future exploits!

Lisa, Gwen, Amoree, Kika, Chris, Cyndi, Kristin, Sherry, Julie, Cindy, Lynne, and Cathy, thank you for keeping my life in balance. My sanity depends on playing with you all!

Even though it would seem like a solo effort, writing a puzzle book relies heavily on teamwork. A very special thanks to Dominique Page, Wendy McAngus, and Carron Brown, my editing team, who were diligent partners in the process. Thanks to illustrator Rhiann Bull and designer Robin Shields who made everything better. And gratitude to Jonathan Bailey, publisher, for taking a chance on me.

First published 2021 by Ammonite, an imprint of Guild of Master Craftsman Publications Ltd
Castle Place, 166 High Street, Lewes,
East Sussex BN7 1XU, UK

Text © Kristy McGowan, 2021
Images © GMC Publications with the exception of the following from Shutterstock.com:
pp35, 70, 90, 100–101, 109, 123, 124, and 125
Copyright in the Work © GMC Publications Ltd, 2021

ISBN 978 1 78145 447 3

Publisher: Jonathan Bailey
Production: Jim Bulley & Jon Hoag
Commissioning & Senior Project Editor: Dominique Page
Senior Project Editor: Wendy McAngus
Technical Editor: Carron Brown
Designer: Robin Shields
Illustrator: Rhiann Bull

Color origination by GMC Reprographics
Printed and bound in China

AMMONITE
PRESS

www.ammonitepress.com